WWII in the Pacific

Great Battles for Boys

Joe Giorello

with
Sibella Giorello

Great Battles World War II in the Pacific

This book is dedicated to Danny Giorello, my dad, who served with the US Army's 15th Air Force, Roger Connor, my father-in-law, who served with the US Navy during the Japanese Occupation, and Jimmy Giorello, my uncle, who served in the US Army Infantry in Europe.

You guys are my heroes.

CONTENTS

Why I Wrote This Book   vii

The Flying Tigers   1

Pearl Harbor   10

Wake Island   19

The Battles of Bataan and Corregidor   28

Next Stop   34

The Bataan Death March   39

The Doolittle Raid   47

The Battle of Midway   56

The Two Battles of Attu   63

The PT Boat   73

Guadalcanal   78

Tarawa   90

The Battle of Saipan   98

The Great Raid   107

Iwo Jima   122

Okinawa   131

The Yamato   140

Victory Over Japan   146

Occupation of Japan   155

Author's Note   160

Bibliography   161

About the Author   163

WHY I WROTE THIS BOOK

Many people assume that because the Allies won WWII, the battles were easy victories.

Nothing could be further from the truth.

Japan was an aggressive and ruthless enemy. Its forces were willing to kill as many people as necessary in order to achieve world domination. Japanese forces were also larger and, in many cases, better trained than the Allied forces.

During WWII, the Allies were the clear underdogs.

But brave soldiers and courageous leaders changed the course of history.

Maybe you've heard someone say, "Freedom isn't free." Do you wonder what they mean? They're saying freedom is bought with the blood of warriors and patriots.

As you read about these battles, I hope you'll come to understand that phrase. And I hope that you will honor those sacrifices and appreciate the freedoms we gained from them.

Let's follow an unforgettable journey into one of the greatest military realms of all time—WWII in the Pacific.

THE FLYING TIGERS

December 1941 – July 1942

3rd Squadron Hell's Angels Flying Tigers over China, photographed in 1942 by AVG
pilot Robert T. Smith

MOST PEOPLE THINK that America joined WWII only after Japan
bombed Pearl Harbor.

Technically, that's true.

But before Japan bombed Hawaii, some daring American
pilots were already shooting Japanese planes out of the sky.

These men were called the Flying Tigers.

For many years before WWII broke out, Japan and China
were at war with each other. Sometimes Japan and China also
fought the Soviet Union. These Sino-Japanese wars, as they

were called, boiled over in 1937. Japan claimed that China fired on its soldiers.

To this day, nobody knows for sure if that claim was true. But Japan used it as an excuse to invade China.

And did they ever invade.

Swift and brutal, the Japanese Imperial Army took over China's busiest port, Shanghai, along with several major cities. Japanese soldiers showed no mercy to the Chinese people. The invasion was so bad that the capture of Nanking—China's capital at the time—became known as "The Rape of Nanking." Thousands of Chinese civilians were tortured, raped, and murdered. How many victims were there? Nobody could ever give an accurate number because the Japanese soldiers destroyed all the records, hoping to avoid war crime convictions.

The invasion was so bad that China pleaded for help. It had a military, headed by General Chiang Kai-Shek. But the Chinese soldiers were no match for the fierce Japanese forces.

So China asked the United States to help. Actually, they asked one particular American—Colonel Claire Lee Chenault.

Colonel Claire Chenault in his office at Kunming, China, 1942

Chenault was an American military man who had worked in China for several years. Just as the Japanese invaded, he was getting ready to retire. But the wife of General Kai-Shek went to him, begging Chenault to build a Chinese air force.

Chenault liked the idea. He thought that a Chinese war with Japan would eventually spread to America, too. So he presented a plan to US President Franklin D. Roosevelt. The only problem was that America wasn't formally at war. So the president couldn't give his official approval. And getting Congress's approval would be difficult.

So a secret plan was made. The president gave Chenault permission to form something called the American Volunteer Group or AVG.

Chenault handpicked about eighty pilots from the American navy, army, and marines. These men then had to resign from active military duty and become mercenaries or "hired guns." They agreed to be part of this covert—secret—operation that wasn't formally recognized by their own government. It was risky.

But some inexperienced pilots wanted to join the AVG so badly that they lied about their flying experience!

One reason they lied was because the AVG paid good money.

During the 1930s, the Great Depression had crippled the American economy. More than 25 percent of Americans didn't have jobs. A pilot joining Chenault's AVG would be paid $600 a month which is about $10,000 in today's dollars! And if a pilot shot down a Japanese plane, he was promised another $500—per plane.

Chenault had his hands full. He had around 300 men who joined. He had to ship everything—all of the pilots, crew, and supplies—to Burma, a country that was friendly to America which also shared a border with China. Then Chenault set up headquarters in a schoolhouse.

Even if they didn't lie about their flying experience, the AVG pilots still had a lot to learn.

AVG pilots and crew working on their planes in Burma

"I gave the pilots a lesson in the geography of Asia that they all needed badly..." Chenault said. "I taught them all I knew about the Japanese. Day after day there were lectures from my notebooks, filled during the previous four years of combat. All of the bitter experience from Nanking to Chunking was poured out in those lectures. Captured Japanese flying and staff manuals, translated into English by the Chinese, served as textbooks. From these manuals the American pilots learned more about Japanese tactics than any single Japanese pilot ever knew."

The Americans were flying P-40 planes which were much faster than the Japanese planes, but the Japanese planes were more maneuverable. So Chenault needed to teach his pilots some lifesaving tactics. For instance, pilots should "dive and zoom" on the enemy. They were to fly head-on, firing guns. When the enemy retreated, the pilots were taught to follow them and harass the pilot far beyond the combat area.

It was nothing like what these pilots had learned back in the United States.

But Chenault knew that the Japanese plane—called the Nate, or KI-27—didn't have armor plating. And their fuel tanks weren't self-sealing. One bullet could blow up the whole plane.

And you know what? Chenault's methods worked. Many years later, a British recovery team dredged the water where the Japanese pilots flew back to base after confronting the AVG. The recovery team found more than sixty Japanese planes all shot down by the Flying Tigers.

Since it was a secret operation, Chenault only had about fifty operational airplanes. But he fooled the Japanese into thinking there were huge numbers of P-40s. One trick was to constantly change the P-40s' paint colors and tail numbers. Chenault did this so often that the Japanese decided there were about 500 AVG planes! To keep up the deception, Chenault's fighter squadrons were taught to attack in groups of three— one plane right, one center, and one left—so that the enemy would think it was a huge fleet.

After suffering for decades under Japanese oppression, the Chinese people celebrated these fierce American pilots. They nicknamed them "Tigers." One pilot decided to paint the nose of his P-40 so it looked like a Tiger shark. Then other pilots did the same thing. When an American reporter came to see these wild mercenaries fighting for China, he added to the nickname, calling them "Flying Tigers."

The name stuck.

Radar systems were a brand new invention at the time. Too new for the Flying Tigers. But the pilots had a different early warning system—the Chinese people.

Every time a Japanese plane took off to attack the AVG, the Chinese people would run from one village to another, searching for a radio, telephone, or telegraph wire to alert the Americans. These early signals prevented Japan from having any element of surprise against the Flying Tigers. Chenault later called this unusual alarm system a "vast spider net."

Also, if an American pilot crashed or was forced to bail out of his plane, he had something called a "blood chit" to save his life. The blood chit was a cloth emblem, written in Chinese, sewn into the pilot's uniforms. It read: "This person has come to China to help in the war effort. Soldiers and civilians, one and all, should rescue and protect him."

Years after WWII, a reporter interviewed AVG pilot RT Smith. He asked him what it was like being a Flying Tiger. Living conditions were rough. Eight pilots died during the secret mission.

"Did you ever regret joining the AVG?" asked the reporter.

Blood chit for a Flying Tiger

Smith said, "Only on those occasions when I was being shot at."

Although eight Flying Tigers lost their lives, the AVG inflicted huge losses on the Japanese. Almost 300 Japanese planes were destroyed, while about 1,500 Japanese aviation personnel were wounded or killed.

But in December 1941, Japan bombed Pearl Harbor.

That caused the United States to bring these daring pilots back into its military.

On July 4, 1942, the AVG was disbanded.

The Tiger pilots were sent into other units, continuing to fight the Japanese—and Germans—in World War II.

WHO FOUGHT?

THE FLYING TIGERS sound like a real success story, doesn't it?

But it didn't start out that way. Some pilots quit after only twenty-four hours in Burma. Others didn't even know how to fly a plane. One pilot crashed three different planes—in one week.

Frustrated, Chenault wrote a letter to the Central Aircraft Manufacturing Company. It was a private business overseeing the AVG since the American government wasn't officially involved. He wrote:

"In telling the A.V.G. story to pilots who may think of volunteering, nothing should be omitted....The A.V.G. will be called upon to combat Japanese pursuits; to fly at night; and to undertake offensive missions when planes suitable for this purpose are sent out to us. These points should be clearly explained.

"Then, after the timid have been weeded out, the incompetents should also be rejected. I am willing to give a certain amount of transition training to new pilots, but we are not equipped to give a complete refresh course. It is too much to expect that men familiar only with four-engine flying boats can be transformed into pursuit experts overnight....

"Let me repeat, much money and much irreplaceable equipment has already been wasted, the A.V.G.'s combat efficient seriously lowered, by the employment policy that has been followed. I am aware that this policy makes it far easier to fill the employment quotas. But I prefer to have the employment quotas partly unfilled, than to receive pilots hired on the principle of 'Come one, come all.' "

You can read all of Chenault's letter here:
www.warbirdforum.com/camco.htm

BOOKS

Flying Tigers by Paul Szuscikiewicz

Claire Chennault: Flying Tiger by Earle Rice

INTERNET

LIFE magazine featured the Flying Tigers in a 1942 issue. The following website link will take you directly to that story, which has many excellent photos of the Flying Tigers and their planes. However, be aware that at that time, Americans used disparaging language to describe their Japanese enemy. www.cbi-theater.com/flyingtigers/flying_tigers.html

MOVIES

Flying Tigers

The Sky's the Limit

God is My Co-Pilot

Hers to Hold

China's Little Devils

PEARL HARBOR

Dec. 7, 1941

The USS *Arizona* burning in Pearl Harbor, Hawaii, Dec. 7, 1941

DECEMBER 7, 1941 was a normal Sunday. Across America, families gathered for breakfast, got ready for church, and listened to their radios playing in the background.

Christmas was just weeks away.

But suddenly an announcer broke into the regular radio program. He said that the Japanese had bombed Pearl Harbor.

Pearl Harbor?

People looked at each other.

Where's Pearl Harbor?

In 1941, Hawaii wasn't even a state. It was only a very distant US territory. But after that fateful December day, everyone knew about the place named Pearl Harbor.

People struggled to understand why the Japanese had attacked American soil. During World War I, Japan was an American ally—a friend—that fought on the side of the US, Great Britain, France, and Italy.

However, Japan just declared itself America's enemy.

What changed?

After WWI, Japan tumbled into a terrible economic depression. Military leaders seized control of the Japanese government. These leaders told people they would make things better. Then Japan brutally attacked China and took over its major ports. (Remember, this was why the Flying Tigers were in Burma.) But the invasion of China wasn't enough power for Japan's new leaders. Especially for the aggressive Minister of War, General Hideki Tojo.

Tojo believed that Japan was a holy country, superior to all others. Most Japanese citizens agreed with him. For centuries, Japanese culture taught its people to believe they were a special race, destined to rule over all the people in Asia. (In Germany, Adolf Hitler used this same sense of superiority to lead his countrymen into WWII).

But there was another reason behind Japan's aggression. Japan is a narrow string of islands in the Pacific Ocean containing millions of people who needed food and other supplies. Japan imported most of its food and raw supplies from other countries. But when Japan invaded China, the United States stopped sending raw materials to them. This embargo was supposed to persuade Japan to leave China alone. But the embargo made Japan's economic problems even worse, so Tojo tried to conquer more territory.

In 1939, Japan attacked the Soviet Union. It didn't win that conflict, but the following year, Japan's leaders signed something called the Pact of Steel. This agreement with Germany and Italy made Japan a member of the Axis alliance. These three countries banded together for power.

In 1941, General Tojo became Prime Minister of Japan. He convinced Japan's royal leader, Emperor Hirohito, that Japan should attack the United States. Tojo said that if Japan didn't show some real muscle, the world would always treat Japan like a third-class country. So Japan planned its attack on the United States at the same time Japanese diplomats were discussing peace terms with the US.

American naval commanders in Hawaii had heard rumors that Japan might attack. But the navy was told to ignore the warnings. The War Department in Washington DC was convinced the diplomatic talks with Japan were genuine, and that Japan was interested in peace. They also said that Japan's military was already overextended and couldn't fight another war.

On December 7, 1941 another message was sent to Washington. It said, Japan was going to attack Pearl Harbor—*today!*

With our modern computers, cell phones, and "instant messaging," it's hard to understand how that message didn't immediately reach Hawaii. But back then, sending a message halfway around the world required hours, sometimes even entire days, to reach its destination.

When the message finally did reach General Walter Short in Hawaii, Pearl Harbor was already in flames.

Here's how the attack took place.

Sunday morning, December 7, 1941, was another sunny day on Oahu island. But the first sign of trouble came at 6:30 a.m. A military spotter saw a Japanese midget submarine operating near the entrance to Pearl Harbor. The midget sub was sunk, and an early warning signal was dispatched.

But the warning was ignored.

Minutes later, the island's radar station signaled a fleet of planes was approaching from about fifty miles away. This information was sent to the army. A commander passed the news to the navy. And the naval officer assumed these planes were a fleet of American B-17 bombers, expected to arrive at Pearl Harbor that same day.

Minutes later, about 200 enemy planes swooped over Pearl Harbor.

Torpedo bombers.

Dive bombers.

Fighter planes.

There were so many planes that they blocked the sun.

Bypassing Pearl Harbor's battleships, the planes headed straight for a nearby airfield. Unfortunately, the US military was more worried about sabotage than any attack from the air, so it had bunched all its planes together on the airfield—to keep them safe. But that "safeguard" gave the Japanese an easy target.

The Japanese destroyed half of the American planes within minutes.

The enemy then headed for the harbor's "Battleship Row." They dropped torpedoes on the USS *Helena*, *Utah*, and *Raleigh*. More Japanese planes flew in from the east, attacking the USS *California*, *Nevada*, *Oklahoma*, and *West Virginia*. One armor-piercing bomb penetrated the forward ammunition magazine of the USS *Arizona*. The ship exploded. That's the explosion seen in the picture at the top of this chapter.

With Pearl Harbor in ruins, the Japanese planes flew away. One pilot telegraphed a message to command: "Tora, Tora, Tora!"

Literally, the phrase translates as "Tiger, Tiger, Tiger!" Or Japanese code for "Surprise attack achieved!"

Only the attack wasn't over.

Another 170 Japanese planes arrived in a second wave. They targeted the ships damaged from the first attack, the battleship *Pennsylvania*, and three destroyers that were in dry dock.

Photo # NH 97398   USS West Virginia sunk and burning at Pearl Harbor, 7 Dec. 1941

Before the morning was over, twenty ships were sunk or ruined. Almost 200 planes were destroyed, another 159 were damaged. Most of them never even left the ground.

In less than two hours, Japan wiped out America's naval force in the Pacific. But human casualties were even higher. The bombing of Pearl Harbor killed about 2,500 Americans, including 68 civilians. The explosion on the USS *Arizona* killed 1,177 crewmen—the highest number of deaths that day on any ship.

And yet, when the smoke cleared, the military saw some good fortune.

Admiral Husband Kimmel had already dispatched every single aircraft carrier to various duties, including delivering fighter planes to the islands named Wake and Midway. That meant all the aircraft carriers survived.

And the Japanese made a serious strategic error. Despite all the planning behind the attack, Japanese bombs didn't hit any fuel storage tanks, maintenance areas, or submarines. Most of America's destroyer ships survived, too.

These errors turned out to be significant.

Until now, most Americans were reluctant to get involved in WWII. In Europe, the war had been raging for several years. But after the attack on Pearl Harbor, Americans wanted retribution.

On December 8, President Roosevelt and Congress declared war on Japan.

Roosevelt called December 7 "a date that will live in infamy."

During the next six months, Japanese military forces would sweep across Asia, invading or attacking Shanghai, Hong Kong, Singapore, Thailand, Malaysia, Burma, the Philippines, the Dutch East Indies, Java, Borneo, Sumatra, New Guinea, Solomon and Gilbert Islands, Wake, Guam, and the Aleutian Islands of Alaska.

The Japanese looked unstoppable.

WHO FOUGHT?

ON THE MORNING of December 7, 1941, Doris "Dorrie" Miller was collecting laundry on the USS *West Virginia* when an alarm sounded. Miller headed for his midship battle station at an anti-aircraft battery magazine.

But a Japanese torpedo had already wrecked the gun.

So Miller ran on deck.

A former boxing champion, and one of the few black Americans in the navy, Miller was ordered to carry wounded sailors to safety. But later another officer ordered him to the bridge—the ship's command center—because the captain was badly wounded. After taking care of the captain, Miller manned a 50-caliber Browning anti-aircraft machine gun. Though he hadn't been trained to operate the powerful gun, Miller made good use of it.

Japanese planes dropped two armor-piercing bombs

through the battleship's deck, and launched five 18-inch aircraft torpedoes into the *West Virginia's* port side. The ship was already flooding. But Miller kept firing at the enemy until he ran out of ammunition. He downed as many as six Japanese planes before the *West Virginia's* crew was ordered to abandon ship.

The *West Virginia* sank to the bottom of the harbor.

Of the 1,541 sailors onboard, 130 were killed, and 52 were wounded.

For his actions, Miller received the Navy Cross. Admiral Chester Nimitz, the Commander in Chief of the Pacific Fleet, personally presented the medal to Miller.

Nimitz said:

"This marks the first time in this conflict that such high tribute has been made in the Pacific Fleet to a member of his race and I'm sure that the future will see others similarly honored for brave acts."

Miller later served on several ships throughout WWII.

He was aboard an American escort carrier on November 24, 1942 when a Japanese submarine fired a single torpedo. The bomb detonated in the ship's magazine, sinking the vessel.

Dorrie Miller was listed among the 646 American sailors who died on that ship.

BOOKS

The Attack on Pearl Harbor: An Interactive History Adventure by Allison Lassieur

A Boy at War: A Novel of Pearl Harbor by Harry Mazer

Remember Pearl Harbor: Japanese And American Survivors Tell Their Stories by Thomas B. Allen

Pearl Harbor: The U.S. Enters World War II by Steve Dougherty

Attack on Pearl Harbor; The True Story of the Day America Entered World War II by Shelley Tanaka and David Craig

INTERNET

The US Navy maintains several websites dedicated to Pearl Harbor's history. You can find first-person survivor stories, photos, and maps that show where the aircraft carriers were on December 7, 1941 on this site: www.history.navy.mil/browse-by-topic/wars-conflicts-and-operations/world-war-ii/1941/pearl-harbor.html

Be sure to read President Roosevelt's speech, given the day after Pearl Harbor was attacked. People often quote his line about "a day that will live in infamy."
www.loc.gov/resource/afc1986022.afc1986022_ms2201/?st=text

The website EyeWitness to History offers still more information about this attack: www.eyewitnesstohistory.com/pearl.htm

MOVIES

From Here to Eternity

In Harm's Way

Tora, Tora, Tora!

WAKE ISLAND

December 8, 1941

Japanese soldiers invading Wake Island

YOU'VE PROBABLY HEARD about the Alamo, that famous battle in Texas when a handful of people took on the mighty Mexican army. The small group of rebels didn't win, but they fought so bravely that people still say, "Remember the Alamo!"

But there's another battle that people call the Alamo of the Pacific—Wake Island.

Wake Island sits in the South Pacific Ocean. Though small, the island was important to Japan. In fact, they wanted Wake so badly that they attacked it the very next day after Pearl Harbor.

Remember how one piece of good fortune for the Americans was that no aircraft carriers were in Pearl Harbor when the Japanese attacked? One of those carriers, the USS *Enterprise*, was actually delivering airplanes to Wake Island, where more than 400 Marines and 1,000 construction crew workers were building an airfield and an American defensive position.

America's military had already sensed Japan's aggression might move toward Wake.

Look at the map below. Wake Island is a horseshoe-shaped coral atoll—or reef. The island is located in the Pacific Ocean about 2,000 miles west of Hawaii, and just north of the Marshall Islands. At the outbreak of WWII, Japan controlled the Marshall Islands.

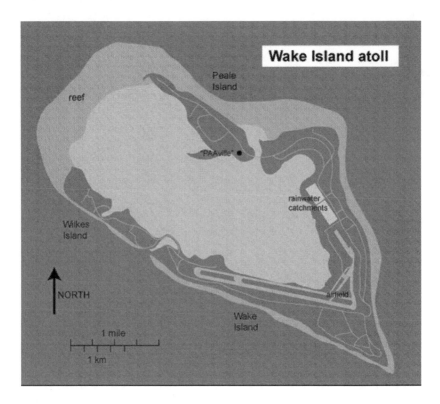

If the Americans could take control of Wake Island, then Allied bombers would be within striking distance of Japanese territory. Of course, Japan wanted to prevent that from happening, so right after attacking Pearl Harbor, Japanese warships sailed for this small island 2,000 miles to the west.

Although the *Enterprise* had delivered twelve F4F-3 Wildcat airplanes to Wake Island, it didn't deliver any radar equipment or any gear that protected the planes from an aerial attack. If those supplies had been delivered, this battle might have ended very differently.

As Pearl Harbor smoldered, the US Navy alerted the commander on Wake Island, Winfield Cunningham. Commander Cunningham ordered four Wildcats to patrol the skies around the island.

But an ocean haze hindered visibility that day, and the pilots had no radar equipment. When they didn't see any enemy planes, the pilots headed back to the airfield.

Suddenly thirty-six Japanese bombers appeared. They dropped their loads on the tiny island, destroying the eight Wildcats still on the ground. The bombs also damaged the airfield, and killed or wounded thirty-four American servicemen.

Japan suffered no losses.

Wrecked U.S. Marine Corps Grumman F4F-3 Wildcat" fighters on Wake Island,
December 1941

Japan's invasion force included six destroyers, two troop
carriers, two armed merchant vessels, one light cruiser, and
more than 1,000 troops.

Japan expected to conquer Wake in no time.

But the 450 US Marines on Wake Island wouldn't let Japan
get away with it.

On December 11th, the fleet of Japanese ships confidently
closed in on the island. Major James Devereux, in charge of the
US marines on Wake, ordered his gunners to hold fire. He
waited until most of the Japanese ships were within range.
Then six coastal artillery guns erupted from "Battery L" on
Peale Island.

The Japanese destroyer *Hayate* was about 4,000 yards out
when it was hit, with at least two hits going directly to the
ship's magazines—where ammunition is stored. The *Hayate*
exploded. Devereux also sent out the four remaining Wildcats.

One plane landed a bomb on the *Hayate's* stern, detonating the storage area filled with depth charges.

Every man onboard the *Hayate* was killed. The Japanese fleet pulled out of range.

It was the first American victory of WWII. It was also the last time in history that onshore guns would repel an attempted invasion.

But the Battle of Wake Island wasn't over.

The Japanese forces weren't leaving. In fact, even more ships were coming—sailing in from the successful attack on Pearl Harbor.

Cunningham and Devereux radioed Hawaii for help.

The American Navy dispatched the carrier USS *Saratoga* from Hawaii. It was carrying forces and supplies. Meanwhile, the marines on Wake stepped up their fight, refusing to back down. Devereux also moved his fortifications from one spot to another, confusing the enemy and preventing the main artery from getting cut off.

On December 22nd, right after days of bombings by Japanese planes, bad news arrived. The US Navy was recalling the *Saratoga*. America had lost too many ships in Pearl Harbor. Seeing Japan's build-up around Wake, the Navy decided it couldn't risk losing another ship.

The men on Wake were on their own.

The marines fought hard, never giving up. At times, the fighting was so fierce that even the construction workers joined in, using shovels or any tool available to beat back the invading enemy forces.

But Devereux realized time wasn't on their side. Two more Wildcats were shot down. And the Japanese invasion fleet had grown even larger with four heavy cruisers and more than

1,500 troops. Devereux wondered how long the Americans could keep the Japanese from overpowering them. His troops were fiercely brave, but they were outnumbered two to one.

On December 23, Devereux and Cunningham suddenly lost radio contact with their forces. They had no way of knowing if the men on Wake's three islands were winning or losing, living or dying. "I tried to think of something we might do to keep going," Devereux later recalled, "but there wasn't anything... We could keep on expending lives, but we could not buy anything with them." Later that same day, Devereux surrendered to the Japanese.

The fifteen-day siege on Wake Island had killed forty-seven marines, three naval personnel, and seventy civilians. Forty-nine marines were wounded, and two were missing.

But even outnumbered, the Americans had killed about 800 Japanese and wounded more than 300. They had also taken out two Japanese destroyers, one submarine, and twenty-one aircraft.

America lost the battle at Wake Island, but reports of the marines' courage and persistence reached other American troops. After the humiliating attack on Pearl Harbor, Americans were inspired by the marines. Instead of saying they lost the battle at Wake Island, people started calling it "the Alamo of the Pacific."

However, tragically, the Japanese captured every American alive on Wake Island. The Americans became prisoners of war, or POWs, sent to Japanese prison camps where they endured brutal treatment.

Ninety-eight civilians were kept on Wake Island as forced labor. Later, the Japanese executed them.

1942 cartoon by Ralph Lee

WHO FOUGHT?

AS A RESULT of lessons learned at Wake Island, civilian construction workers serving in the armed forces were trained in weaponry and basic tactics. Eventually these men became known as the Naval Construction Battalion, or "Seabees," from the initials C.B. Seabees were a tough group. Some of them had worked in mines and quarries and wharfs. Others built America's skyscrapers and subways. Seabees covered more than sixty skilled trades.

By the end WWII, about 325,000 men were enlisted in the Seabees. They built more than 100 airstrips, 400 piers, 2,500 ammunition magazines, 700 square blocks of warehouses, hospitals to serve 70,000 patients, tanks for the storage of

100,000,000 gallons of gasoline, and housing for 1,500,000 men. And that was only in the Pacific.

Roughly 200 Seabees died in combat. They also earned about 2,000 Purple Hearts, 33 Silver Stars, and 5 Navy Crosses.

On Wake Island, the construction workers did everything from dredging the channel to building the naval air station.

The ninety-eight men kept as forced labor on Wake were later lined up by the Japanese and machine-gunned to death.

But one Seabee managed to escape. He's believed to have carved his initials into a nearby coral rock, documenting the ninety-eight who died. The Japanese later captured him and allegedly beheaded him.

But "98 Rock" remains on Wake Island to this day.

BOOKS

Wake Island 1941: A Battle to Make the Gods Weep by Jim Moran.

INTERNET

This brief video shows a dogfight between a Japanese Zero and a US F6F Hellcat as it would have occurred in the raid on Wake Island: history.com/videos/raid-on-wake-island#raid-on-wake-island

The *Atlantic* magazine published some vivid photographs of WWII in the Pacific: www.theatlantic.com/infocus/2011/09/world-war-ii-the-pacific-islands/100155

Want to know more about the American Marines? The National Museum of the Marine Corps offers information on the Corps: www.usmcmuseum.com/lore-of-the-corps.html

MOVIES

Wake Island: Alamo of the Pacific

Fighting Seabees

THE BATTLES OF BATAAN AND CORREGIDOR

December 8, 1941

Japanese tanks rolling over Bataan

YOU ALREADY KNOW that Japan hit Wake Island within hours of destroying Pearl Harbor. But Japan also quickly attacked the Philippine Islands, too, where thousands of American service personnel were stationed under the command of General Douglas MacArthur.

Fortunately, after WWI, the United States began planning for a possible Japanese invasion of the Philippines. The plan, devised by both the US Navy and Army, was called War Plan Orange. Its purpose was to protect the 45,000 troops stationed in these islands.

Unfortunately, War Plan Orange had one big flaw. It depended on an air fleet and reinforcements arriving from Pearl Harbor.

But Japan had wiped out both planes and troops in their sneak attack on Hawaii, and now, the day after Pearl Harbor, Japanese planes swooped over the Philippines, destroying half of General MacArthur's fleet of B-17 bombers and P-40 fighters. Once again, most of the planes never even left the ground.

The attack continued for five days.

Philippine navy yard fire following Japanese air raid, December 10, 1941

Before December was over, Japanese General Masaharu Homma was landing troops on the island of Luzon, where most of the Americans were stationed. Homma cleverly placed his troops in three different locations, hoping to encircle MacArthur's forces.

Realizing his new predicament, MacArthur withdrew his entire force, which included about 65,000 native Filipinos fighting with the Americans. MacArthur sent them all to the Bataan Peninsula on Luzon's south end. MacArthur hoped to launch the rest of War Plan Orange from there, positioning his defensive lines in five different locations. Each line was one day's march from the next.

On paper, War Plan Orange looked brilliant. But this sudden withdrawal to Bataan meant leaving behind supplies that the troops desperately needed—food, fresh water, ammunition, gasoline, and medical supplies. Meanwhile, the plan called for the troops being able to hold out for six months. That time frame suddenly looked very uncertain, especially with Japanese warships encircling the islands, blocking any help or supplies from reaching the Americans.

Another difficulty during this invasion came from the Americans themselves. Although 30,000 army and marine personnel and 15,000 air force fighters sounds like a large force, it wasn't nearly enough to defend against the massive Japanese military. Moreover, the native Filipinos fighting alongside the Americans were poorly trained and lacked modern weapons. One-quarter of the Filipino hand grenades failed to ignite. Two-thirds of their mortar rounds were duds.

The Japanese forces marched toward these men—isolated on a southern stretch of the island.

Within a month, the lack of supplies left the Americans suffering from hunger and exhaustion.

Japanese flame-thrower assaulting a bunker during the Battle of Bataan

On January 8, Japanese forces assaulted the eastern flank of a defensive line. But the Army's 91st Division and the 57th Infantry pushed back. Alexander R. Nininger Jr., platoon leader of the 57th, fought his way into Japanese foxholes, armed only with a rifle and hand grenades. In hand-to-hand combat against the enemy, Nininger helped his unit retake the line.

When Japanese forces burst through the tropical foliage, Filipino fighter Narcisco Ortilano fired a heavy machine gun until it died. He then grabbed his .45 pistol and kept shooting. One Japanese soldier stabbed Ortilano with a bayonet, but Ortilano continued trying to grab the enemy's gun, even after the soldier sliced off his thumb. Ortilano finally stabbed the enemy in the chest, swinging the bayonet just as another Japanese soldier came upon him. Ortilano shot him dead.

Through January and February, the Japanese continued their attacks. The Americans fought relentlessly. But food was running low. The Americans were placed on quarter-rations, meaning one half-meal a day. The extreme hunger drove men to eat the mules that died in battle. Other men suffered from tropical diseases such as malaria and dysentery which meant that even standing up was a struggle.

Meanwhile, Japan continued sending fresh reinforcements into the battle.

Back in Washington DC, President Roosevelt grew concerned. MacArthur was America's most experienced general in the Pacific, but he could not win against the Japanese. Roosevelt ordered MacArthur to leave the Philippines. MacArthur resisted until March 12th when the general, his family, and some other officers were shipped to Australia aboard some Patrol Transport (PT) boats.

Lieutenant General Jonathan Wainwright was placed in command.

The Americans still refused to give up. Frustrated by such fierce resistance, Japan added 190 artillery pieces, including field howitzers and 150mm cannons.

On April 3, from 9:00 a.m. to 3:00 p.m., Japan bombed one side of the Bataan Peninsula to the other. Some parts of the island became infernos. During the next three days—from Good Friday to Easter Sunday—Japanese tanks and infantry attacked what remained of the defensive lines.

Though weak and ravaged, the American forces pushed back.

Japan crushed their every maneuver.

On April 7, American commanders lost contact with their forces. The roads around Bataan became clogged with fleeing refugees and retreating Filipino troops. Field commander General Edward King saw his troops so weakened by months of hunger, disease, and nonstop fighting that the men could barely lift their rifles.

On April 8, disobeying orders, King discussed terms of surrender with Japan.

General Homma refused to accept terms. Either the Americans surrendered unconditionally or the battle continued.

On April 9, realizing this fight could not be won, General King surrendered.

But the fight wasn't over.

NEXT STOP

CORREGIDOR

The Malinta Tunnel in Corregidor during the Battle of Bataan

JUST OFF THE southern tip of the Bataan Peninsula, sits the island of Corregidor. It was called "The Rock."

As Japanese forces stormed down the peninsula, America's main command moved to Corregidor—specifically to Malinta Hill, a tunnel complex. Built in the 1920s, the underground village was large enough to hold the army command center, barracks, a hospital, storage facilities, and even an officer's club.

On April 9, when King surrendered Bataan, Japanese forces immediately headed for The Rock. They used more than seventy-five heavy artillery pieces to rain explosive terror on Corregidor.

Inside the tunnel, life turned grim.

Drinking water supplies were running low. Communications came in sporadic bursts. The constant bombardment by the Japanese shook the dugout walls. Surgeons resorted to flashlights because lights inside the tunnel flickered on and off.

The Japanese fired 16,000 artillery rounds in one day.

By early May, the American defenses were down to just a few machine gun positions and two coastal guns.

The Japanese tanks roared across the island and stopped at the tunnel's entrance.

Inside, more than 1,000 wounded men lay in the underground hospital. General Wainwright knew that if these Japanese tanks fired on the tunnel's entrance, the resulting fireball would incinerate everyone inside. And fighting outside had been reduced to hand-to-hand combat.

Wainwright sent out runners, telling the American soldiers to destroy all their weapons.

Marine Private Ernest J. Bales was furious. "Was this what we'd spent all these damned days and nights dodging bombs for?" he later said. "I couldn't believe it."

Wainwright also wrote to President Roosevelt. "It is with broken heart and head bowed in sadness, but not in shame, that I report to Your Excellency that I must go today to arrange terms for the surrender of the fortified islands of Manila Bay... There is a limit of human endurance, and that limit has long since been passed... Goodbye, Mr. President."

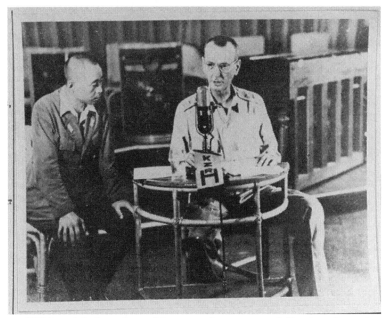

General Wainwright broadcasts his surrender message, following the capture of
Corregidor by the Japanese, May 1942

Japan demanded unconditional surrender. Wainwright wanted to avoid that because American troops were still fighting in other parts of the Philippines. Unconditional surrender would mean Japan had total control of all the islands. But, with flame-throwing tanks stationed at the tunnel's entrance, Wainwright didn't have much choice.

"I was desperately cornered," he later said. "My troops on Corregidor were almost completely disarmed, as well as wholly isolated from the outside world."

Wainwright agreed to unconditional surrender. "That was it," he said. "The last hope vanished from my mind."

As Wainwright was taken from the tunnel by Japanese guards, he passed by hundreds of his men. Wounded, defeated, dying, they tried to console him. "It's all right, General," they said. "You did your best."

Private Edward Reamer stood near Wainwright as he was

taken away.

"I could see tears on Wainwright's cheeks," he said. "You couldn't look in any direction outside the tunnel without seeing a dead body. One guy was holding a Tommy gun with half his head blown off. Those guys fought right up to the tunnel, right up to the headquarters."

After nearly five months of fighting, The Battle of Corregidor ended on May 7, 1942.

Wainwright, along with the other American forces, was taken to a Japanese prison camp.

He would remain a POW for the rest of WWII.

WHO FOUGHT?

DOUGLAS MACARTHUR WAS probably the most famous—and most controversial—general of WWII.

Raised in the military, MacArthur graduated first in his class at the West Point Military Academy. He immediately joined the US Army and quickly rose through the ranks, serving during WWI. In 1924, he was sent to the Philippines to quell a rebellion.

In 1937, MacArthur retired from the army and became a military advisor to the Philippine government. But in 1941, the US Army withdrew MacArthur and named him commander of the forces in the Far East.

That same year Japan attacked the Philippines.

After President Roosevelt pulled MacArthur from the Philippines during the Battle of Bataan, many servicemen resented the general leaving the battlefield. MacArthur realized their feelings, and soon after his departure gave a speech. It's known as the "I Shall Return" speech:

"The President of the United States ordered me to break

through the Japanese lines and proceed from Corregidor to Australia for the purpose, as I understand it, of organizing the American offensive against Japan, a primary objective of which is the relief of the Philippines. I came through and I shall return."

General Douglas MacArthur (wearing sunglasses, front and center) upon his return to the Philippines during WWII

BOOKS

Baby of Bataan: Memoir of a 14 Year Old Soldier in World War II by Joseph Quitman Johnson

Resolve: From the Jungles of WW II Bataan, The Epic Story of a Soldier, a Flag, and a Promise Kept by Bob Welch

Douglas MacArthur: Brilliant General, Controversial Leader by Ann Graham Gaines

MOVIES

Bataan

Back to Bataan

Corregidor

THE BATAAN DEATH MARCH

April 9, 1942

American prisoners carry comrades too sick to walk. This photo was among the few taken of the Bataan Death March.

HAVE YOU EVER heard of the Geneva Convention? It's an agreement between warring countries stating that they will not harm defenseless people, including prisoners, during the war.

One part of the Geneva Convention reads, "prisoners of war... must at all times be humanely treated and protected particularly against acts of violence, insults and public curiosity. Measures of reprisal against them are prohibited."

More than forty-five countries signed an updated Geneva Convention treatise after the bloody battles of World War I. Japan signed the agreement, too. But they refused to obey the rules.

Remember that Japanese leaders taught the people that they were a superior race. That culture also believed in the Bushido code. Known as "the warrior's way," the Bushido code laid out the Japanese standard of honor for soldiers, including requiring captured soldiers to commit suicide rather than be at the mercy of their enemies.

The Japanese people had been taught the Bushido code for hundreds of years. The Geneva Convention was only fifteen years old.

Japanese soldiers saw any captured prisoners as dishonorable. Cowardly men who "allowed" themselves to become prisoners. A disgrace to their country's honor.

The American forces that surrendered at Bataan were already skin and bones from months of hunger and nonstop fighting. And the nearly 100,000 American and Filipino men were taken prisoner by the brutal Japanese army.

The Japanese force-marched the POWs fifty-five miles up the Bataan Peninsula to the city of San Fernando.

American prisoners of war with their hands tied behind their backs, during the Bataan Death March. They are identified as (L to R): Samuel Stenzler, Frank Spear & James Gallagher. *US Marine Corps photo.*

In April, the tropical weather was hot and humid. As the march continued, mile after mile, the POWs continually dropped to the ground from exhaustion, hunger, thirst, and disease. Many POWs were suffering from malaria, a mosquito-borne illness that causes extreme flu-like symptoms. Others had dysentery from unclean water and suffered crippling stomach pains and diarrhea that led to further dehydration and even death.

The Japanese soldiers refused to give the POW's fresh water. They even poured out the water from inside the Americans' canteens. If a prisoner asked for water, he was beaten or killed. When a prisoner fell to the ground or slowed down the march in any way, he was beaten or stabbed with bayonets.

Day after day, the march continued, and the Japanese soldiers found new ways to inflict suffering on the POWs.

"Their ferocity grew as we marched," recalled POW Captain William Dyess, squadron commander of the 21st Pursuit. "They were no longer content with mauling stragglers or pricking them with bayonet points. The thrusts were intended to kill."

Private Blair Robinett of Company C 803rd Engineers watched one Japanese soldier pick up a sick POW and throw him into the path of some oncoming tanks.

"When the last tank left, there was no way you could tell there'd ever been a man there. But his uniform was embedded in the cobblestone."

Over the course of the fifty-five-mile trek, some Filipino civilians tried to give the POWs water and food. But the Japanese soldiers beat and killed those people too.

Six days later, the POWs reached San Fernando. The survivors were loaded into metal boxcars.

Each car was only big enough for about forty men, but the Japanese stuffed more than hundred men into each car. Then they closed the doors and a train carried the cars down the tracks. The airless containers, baked by the hot sun, filled with a poisonous stench. Dysentery affected so many POWs that soon the rail car floor was slick with mucus, blood, and excrement. Men were packed so tightly they remained upright even after they died from suffocation.

Miles later, the POWs were unloaded.

The dead men were left behind. The living were force-marched another eight miles to Camp O'Donnell.

Of the 100,000 POWs who started the march in Bataan, only 54,000 reached Camp O'Donnell. Some 10,000 Filipinos died on the march, and some 600 Americans. Other prisoners escaped, slipping away into the jungle where they continued to fight the Japanese as guerrilla warriors.

The torture continued at Camp O'Donnell.

The POWs were stripped of their possessions. If a soldier had any Japanese items or money, he was executed on the spot. The Japanese soldiers confiscated everything from blankets and pens to surgical equipment and knives. The only items the POWs were allowed to keep were their canteens, their mess kits holding rations, and a metal plate and spoon.

With only two water spigots for 53,000 men, the line to fill the canteens was sometimes twelve hours long. Desperate for something to quench their thirst, men pulled water from a nearby river. But it was polluted and caused even more dysentery to break out. The only latrines consisted of trenches in the ground. Sick men were unable to control their bowels while waiting in line. Many prisoners resorted to using buckets as toilets. Flies landed on the excrement and carried the disease further, eventually contaminating the food supply.

The camp had no effective dysentery medicine. The sick men were placed in separate barracks, which became waiting rooms for death.

Within the first forty days of arriving, 1,570 Americans died at Camp O'Donnell. Some succumbed to illness, others died from the savage beatings of their captors.

Soon the men captured at Corregidor joined these men at the camp.

But in July 1942, the Japanese transferred all POWs except the very sickest to another camp called Cabanatuan. Some 3,000 POWs died there.

But most Americans back home heard nothing about the Bataan Death March until about two years later in 1944. The military released sworn statements by some officers who had escaped the march. After hearing of the Japanese brutality against POWs, Americans felt renewed passion to win this war.

American POW executed on Bataan Death March

WHO FOUGHT?

PRIVATE LEON BECK of the 31st Infantry Battalion was on the Bataan Death March. He survived to tell his story:

"I don't think there's any glory in being a prisoner of war, and I'd made up my mind, when it looked desperate... I told everybody: 'I'm not going to march in the prison camp. If I have to die, I'm going to die in the attempt or I'll die free. But I'm not going to go in prison camp, no glory in being a prisoner.' We were taught [that] you had a moral, legal, and ethical responsibility if you were ever captured, that you should make an attempt to escape and if that attempt was successful, you had to continue to resist your enemy, until such time as you could re-join friendly forces. You had to continue to resist your enemy. That's the way it was taught to us, every time they read the Articles of War to us. So, I've tried to fulfill that. I enlisted voluntarily and I felt I had a responsibility and I tried to fulfill it."

How did Beck escape the Death March?

"The road that we were marching on was the main road from Manila all the way into Bataan, to Baguio, which was the summer capital. And, as we came in to the town of Geauga, there was a tide river, that paralleled the road. And nobody would go with me, I'd been begging for many days for people to attempt an escape with me. And, they just flat refused... [Finally] I said 'hit it.' I just rolled off of the road and got into the edge of the river and there's a lot of palmetto brush and weeds and one thing or another growing and as soon as the group marched on past me, and got a ways down the road, and out of sight and there wasn't anything in sight, coming up the road, I went up, swam and waded across that river and got out into a cut rice field and I could see a shack over there..."

After his daring escape, Beck was helped by Filipino civilians who nursed him back to health. He then joined the American guerillas and continued to fight the Japanese in the Philippines.

You can read more of Private Beck's story and others who survived the Death March here:
www.pbs.org/wgbh/americanexperience/features/macarthur
-siege-bataan

BOOKS

A Study in Valor: The Faith of a Bataan Death March Survivor by
William T. Garner

The Bataan Death March: World War II Prisoners in the Pacific (Snapshots in History) by Robert Greenberger

Voices of the Pacific: Untold Stories from the Marine Heroes of World War II by Adam Makos, Marcus Brotherton

INTERNET

The National Museum of the US Air Force maintains several links to Bataan Death March sites: www.nationalmuseum.af.mil/Visit/Museum-Exhibits/Fact-Sheets/Display/Article/196214/imperial-brutality-bataan-death-march

MOVIES

Bataan

Back to Bataan

THE DOOLITTLE RAID

April 18, 1942

B-25 launching of the USS *Hornet*

JAPAN WAS WINNING every battle.

The United States Navy knew that it needed to turn this war around or America would be hit hard.

The Navy needed a bold attack—something to stun Japan.

They decided to bomb Tokyo, Japan's capital city.

That would send a powerful message.

Today we have airplanes and high-tech weapons that can easily accomplish that mission. But in 1942, bombing Tokyo looked almost impossible. Japan was thousands of miles from the nearest American air base. No bomber plane could hold enough fuel to fly all the way to Tokyo, drop its load, and fly home to safety.

For any pilot, that mission would be a suicide run.

But then Navy Captain Francis Low came up with an idea. What if America could get an aircraft carrier close to Japan, and then launch planes from the ship's deck?

Nobody had done that before.

On February 2, 1942, a B-25 bomber rumbled on the deck of the USS *Hornet*. The pilot shoved the engine to full throttle, released the brake, and ripped the plane down the deck—straight for the ocean.

But amazingly, at the last moment, the heavy plane lifted like a bird, clearing the water.

After that successful launch, the Navy was confident this same plane could complete the mission to Tokyo. Traveling at a maximum speed of 284 miles per hour, the B-25 could carry a bomb load of 3,200 pounds. It also came equipped with six 50-caliber machine guns. Two guns fired forward, two fired from the top turret, and two shot from the tail.

The Navy chose Lieutenant Colonel James Doolittle for this top secret mission, along with an all-volunteer group of pilots and crew. These men would later be known as the Doolittle Raiders. But at that time they volunteered, they knew nothing about their mission. It was so top secret that it was even hidden from many people working inside the military.

Japan had the element of surprise at Pearl Harbor. This time it was America's turn to surprise them.

In mid-April, the USS *Hornet* was sent to within about 500 miles of the Japanese home islands (see map below). The plan was for sixteen bombers to launch on the night of April 18, flying under cover of darkness. They would then attack Japanese military bases and supply chains in the cities of Tokyo, Yokosuka, and Osaka-Kobe.

After dropping their loads, the B-25 pilots would then fly south along the Japanese coast until they reached China. They would refuel before reaching their final destination in Burma. To extend their fuel capacity, the Doolittle Raiders pulled out the two tail guns and replaced them with broomsticks, painted black to fool the enemy into thinking they were still real guns.

Everything seemed ready. But on the morning of April 18, a Japanese fishing boat spotted the American carrier task force. The radio operators stationed on the *Hornet* picked up the fishing boat's signal codes being sent to Japan's Fifth Naval Fleet. The message read: "Three enemy carriers sighted at our position 650 nautical miles east of Inubo Saki at 0630."

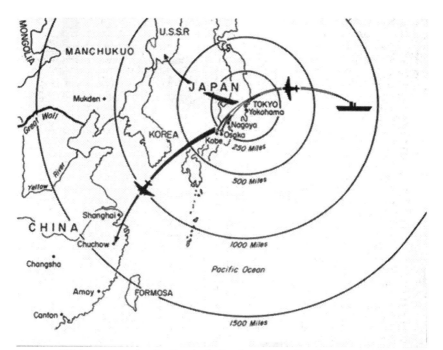

Flight pattern for the Doolittle Raiders to reach safety in China

The element of surprise was gone, and the American naval commanders faced a terrible dilemma.

Should the mission continue?

Not only were the Americans close enough to Japan that Japanese bombers could hit them, the American pilots were looking at a totally different flight. They were still a full day away from where the launch was supposed be. None of the B-25s could carry enough fuel to leave from this location and still reach safety in China.

From the deck of the *Enterprise*, Navy Admiral William "Bull" Halsey blinker-lit a message to the Doolittle Raiders aboard the *Hornet*:

LAUNCH PLANES.

TO COL. DOOLITTLE AND GALLANT COMMAND: GOOD LUCK AND GOD BLESS YOU.

Colonel Doolittle called his pilots on deck.

"If there's any of you who don't want to go, just tell me," he said. "Because the chances of you making it back are pretty slim."

No pilot refused the mission.

And then at 8:15 a.m., the weather turned. Wind whipped across the deck, blowing sheets of rain. High waves splashed over the ship.

The ship's crew decided to use these challenges to their advantage, turning the carrier into the wind. The launch officer timed the waves with the boat pitching up and down. At just the right moment, he snapped his flag.

GO!

Colonel Doolittle was flying the first plane. He yanked the yoke so far back it hit his stomach. Full throttle, full flaps,

Doolittle raced the bomber down the carrier's deck. As the *Hornet* rose on a wave, the head wind slipped under the bomber's wings, lifting it up through the heavy rain.

All sixteen planes made their launch.

What they didn't know was that the message from the fishing vessel did reach the Japanese military. But it never occurred to anyone that bombers could be launched from the carrier, especially in that kind of storm.

The Raiders got another lucky break that morning. Japanese cities were practicing air raid drills and had taken down the barrage balloons that normally floated over the cities to protect them from low-flying attacks.

The bombers had a clear route ahead to the cities. Each B-25 dropped four 500-pound bombs on their intended targets. The damage was serious, but even more powerful was the shock of the attack.

Japan was hit on their home turf.

After dropping their loads, the Doolittle Raiders headed south along the Japanese coastline, praying to reach safety. But the lack of fuel forced eleven crews to bail out, parachuting into unknown and even hostile territory. Four crews crash landed. One plane wound up in Russia.

Among the eighty men who flew off the *Hornet* that morning, ten Raiders were killed. Three were executed after being captured by the Japanese. One died in a Japanese prison camp. Bailouts and crash landings killed the others.

Fourteen crews survived.

Unfortunately, there were even more casualties for the Chinese people. In retaliation for helping save the lives of the American pilots, Japan executed as many as 250,000 Chinese.

But the Doolittle Raid changed the tone of the war. When

news reached the Americans back home, people cheered. This brave mission gave them hope. And pride. Who would ever think of daring to launch planes from a ship?

America proved to her allies—particularly Great Britain—that she was in this fight to win.

For Japan, the raid inflicted tremendous psychological trauma. Its leaders worried that America would keep bombing its cities. As a result, they brought back some elite fighting units from the front lines to defend the main islands. Japan felt vulnerable.

Because none of his planes made it back, Colonel Doolittle thought he was going to be court-martialed for this mission. Instead, he was given the Medal of Honor and promoted to brigadier general. Someone asked President Roosevelt where this raid on Tokyo was launched. His answer was coy. He didn't want anyone to know. There was a popular novel back then called *Lost Horizon* about a fictional paradise named "Shangri-La." So President Roosevelt joked that the Doolittle planes had launched from Shangri-La.

Later, the Navy named one of its aircraft carriers the USS *Shangri-La*.

WHO FOUGHT?

BEFORE LEADING THE legendary raid, James Doolittle was already a famous pilot.

In 1922, he made an astounding cross-country flight. Piloting a DE Havilland DH-4, he flew from Florida all the way to California. In those days, most people didn't even *drive* across the country. Doolittle made only one refueling stop, completing the trip in 21 hours and 19 minutes.

It was the first of his many pioneering flights.

Doolittle was also influential in the aviation industry. Today, pilots fly by instruments alone, but a hundred years ago they had only their eyes. As planes became faster and more maneuverable, the pilots struggled with disorientation, confused by what they saw and what was really there. Doolittle was among the first aviators to recognize the need for cockpit instruments that would help pilots navigate through fog, storms, darkness, and anything else that could hinder their vision.

In 1929, Doolittle was the first pilot to take off, fly, and land an airplane just using instruments with no view from outside the cockpit. He also helped develop technology that is now used in every plane—an artificial horizon and directional gyroscope.

In 1932, Doolittle set the world's high-speed record, flying 296 miles per hour. After winning three air racing trophies, he officially retired.

"I have yet to hear anyone engaged in this work dying of old age," he said.

However, in 1940, he returned to active duty with the armed forces.

Leading the famous Raid, Doolittle and his plane crew were forced to bail out over China, when their plane ran out of fuel—at night in the middle of a storm. Doolittle couldn't locate any kind of landing field, so he put the plane down in a rice paddy. He and his crew were helped by some Chinese guerrillas as well as a famous American missionary named John Birch.

Doolittle continued to fly combat missions as commander of the 12th Air Force in North Africa. He was awarded four Air Medals.

Doolittle received the Medal of Honor for planning and leading the raid on Japan. The citation read:

"For conspicuous leadership above and beyond the call of duty, involving personal valor and intrepidity at an extreme hazard to life. With the apparent certainty of being forced to land in enemy territory or to perish at sea, Lt. Col. Doolittle personally led a squadron of Army bombers, manned by volunteer crews, in a highly destructive raid on the Japanese mainland."

BOOKS

The First Heroes: The Extraordinary Story of the Doolittle Raid—America's First World War II Victory by Craig Nelson

The Doolittle Raid 1942: America's first strike back at Japan by Clayton Chun

Jimmy Doolittle A Short Biography for Kids by Joseph Madden

INTERNET

YouTube has a wonderful five-minute clip on the Doolittle Raid: youtube.com/watch?v=yHnwxRfzR2A

One of the Doolittle Raiders' son maintains a website dedicated to these brave men: www.doolittleraider.com

Naval History and Heritage Command offers some great photographs of the Doolittle Raiders taking off from the aircraft carrier USS *Hornet*: www.history.navy.mil/content/history/nhhc/browse-by-topic/wars-conflicts-and-operations/world-war-ii/1942/halsey-doolittle-raid.html

Here's a link to the USS *Hornet* museum: www.uss-hornet.org

MOVIES

Thirty Seconds Over Tokyo

The Purple Heart

THE BATTLE OF MIDWAY

June 3 – 5, 1942

US Navy Douglas SBD-3 Dauntless dive bombers approach the burning Japanese cruiser *Mikuma* on June 6, 1942. Note bombs hanging under the planes.

LET'S SAY YOU play on a football team. Your next opponent is known for playing rough. They even break the rules and get away with it. But one day you discover their playbook. Now you know all their plans. No matter what dirty trick they try, you'll be onto them.

That's a big advantage for you.

And that's close to what happened when American intelligence officer Captain Joseph Rochefort broke Japan's secret code. Suddenly the Americans knew all about Japan's secret plans, including a mission to attack the island of Midway.

Midway Island was crucial for Japan because of its location.

By taking this island east of its homeland and west of Hawaii, Japan could create a protective defensive zone. And since Japan still didn't know where the Doolittle Raiders took off from, they wanted to make sure Midway wasn't used for another bombing run.

Like Wake Island, Midway is a small string of coral atolls. The total land area is only about three square miles.

But to capture it, Japan had to destroy America's carrier fleet. Admiral Isoroku Yamamoto devised a two-step strategy: Operation AL and Operation MI.

Operation AL was a diversionary attack. Japanese ships would sail north to Alaska, with Japanese soldiers invading the Aleutian Islands. Japan believed America would rush into the fight in Alaska because the enemy would be at its doorstep. That would mean fewer American ships and troops would be available to fight at Midway.

Operation MI focused on Midway. Yamamoto's plan called for four Japanese carriers and eighty support ships to surround the atoll. Japanese planes would bomb the American defenses while invading soldiers would land on two of the atolls then establish a Japanese air base.

Yamamoto expected American carriers to sail into the fight, so he had a fleet of Japanese subs waiting for them. He believed the subs could delay—maybe even destroy—the American ships. Even if American carriers made it to Midway, they would arrive too late to beat Japan's superior air power.

At this point in the war, Japan was winning most of the

Pacific battles. If they secured Midway, they could rule all of Asia.

Yamamoto was so confident of his plan that he expected America to sue for peace. "Suing for peace" means one country starts the peace process, hoping to avoid an unconditional surrender.

But Yamamoto's plan had some flaws.

First, he thought the American carrier *Yorktown* had sunk in an earlier fight, the Battle of the Coral Sea. Instead, repair crews at Pearl Harbor had worked around the clock to put the *Yorktown* back in action, joining carriers *Enterprise* and *Hornet*.

Yamamoto also didn't know that the Japanese code was broken.

When American Admiral Chester Nimitz learned about Yamamoto's plan, he quickly devised a strategic defense for Midway. Nimitz's attitude was "the best defense is a good offense." So instead of waiting for the Japanese forces to hit first, Nimitz decided to ambush them.

First Nimitz sent the *Yorktown, Enterprise*, and *Hornet* north of Midway.

Then, on June 3, American planes attacked the Japanese fleet that was about 600 miles west of Midway. American bombers leaving from Midway joined in the attack. But they scored no damage on the Japanese carriers. Japanese aircraft, such as the Zero, were quick and agile, and their pilots were so aggressive that they forced the B-17 bombers to drop their loads from about 20,000 feet, far too high for the bombs to do much destruction.

The next morning, Japanese Admiral Nagumo sent aircraft to bomb Midway.

But he didn't realize those three American carriers were

waiting for him.

After an initial attack that didn't do much damage, the Japanese planes flew back to their carriers to reload for the next attack. An American observer plane followed the fleet and relayed the precise location of the Japanese carriers back to American commanders.

The Japanese crews aboard the ships were reloading the planes, packing them with bombs for Midway, when American Rear Admirals Raymond Spruance and Jack Fletcher launched torpedo planes from the *Enterprise, Hornet,* and *Yorktown.*

The Japanese managed to shoot down some of the American planes before they could inflict much damage. A second American attack also failed and resulted in the loss of all fifteen planes from one torpedo squadron.

Now the Americans had lost their bomber planes, and Japan knew the exact location of the American carriers.

Hoping to destroy all three ships, Admiral Nagumo ordered his aircrew to change armaments, switching from bombs to torpedoes. But changing armaments delayed takeoff. And in the rush, the bombs were left on the ship's deck, next to the fully-fueled airplanes.

American pilots flying Dauntless dive bombers struck hard, dropping their explosive loads right down the Japanese carriers' exposed elevator shafts.

The explosions destroyed the Japanese ships. Within five minutes, three Japanese carriers—*Akagi, Kaga,* and *Soryu*—were sinking. A fourth carrier, *Hiryu,* stationed about forty miles away from the main battle, managed to cripple the *Yorktown.* But the American planes swooped down for counterstrikes.

The *Hiryu* sank the next day.

One Japanese submarine fired in retaliation, hitting the already-damaged *Yorktown*. The *Yorktown* sank the following day, June 6.

But in just three days, the less-experienced, less-powerful American force had inflicted terrible damages to the Japanese navy. Japan hadn't lost a naval battle in almost eighty years. Now four Japanese aircraft carriers were gone, along with scores of planes and hundreds of highly-trained sailors and pilots. There were not enough men to replace them, and Japan didn't have enough raw materials to rebuild the huge ships.

America had won the Battle of Midway. However, the war was far from over.

Japan stepped up its pounding fight through the Pacific.

Douglas Devastators of Torpedo Squadron 6 on the deck of USS *Enterprise* prior to launching attack against four Japanese carriers in the Battle of Midway

WHO FOUGHT?

LIEUTENANT COMMANDER C. Wade McClusky led the American squadrons that searched the ocean for the Japanese ships that were coming to attack Midway.

Although American intelligence officials gave him a location where the ships were supposed to be, McClusky's squadron found nothing but water.

With his planes running low on fuel, McClusky ordered his pilots to continue searching. Using sly navigational expertise, McClusky eventually found the ships and told his dive bombers to attack. These pilots destroyed the Japanese carriers *Kaga* and *Akagi*.

McClusky's perseverance, said Admiral Nimitz, "decided the fate of our carrier task force and our forces at Midway..."

McClusky, who was awarded the Navy Cross, later described the attack.

"...as I raised my head from the plotting board, a stream of tracer bullets started chopping the water around the plane. Almost immediately my gunner, W. G. Chochalousek, in the rear seat, opened fire. Then a Jap Zero zoomed out of range ahead of me. A hurried glance around found another Zero about 1,000 feet above, to the left and astern, about to make another attack. Remaining at 20 feet above the water, I waited until the attacking plane was well in his dive, then wrapped my plane in a steep turn toward him. This not only gave him a more difficult deflection shot, but also enabled my gunner to have free room to maneuver his guns. Then ensued about a 5-minute chase, first one Zero attacking from the right, then the second from the left. Each time I would wrap up toward the attacker with Chochalousek keeping up a constant fire. Suddenly a burst from a Jap seemed to envelop the whole plane. The left side of my cockpit was shattered, and I felt my left shoulder had been hit with a sledgehammer. Naturally enough it seemed like the end, we sure were goners. After two or three seconds, I realized there was an unusual quietness except for the purring engine of the old Dauntless. Grasping the inner phone, I yelled to Chochalousek, but no answer. It was difficult to turn with the pain in my left shoulder and arm, but I finally managed and there was the gunner. Facing aft, guns at the ready and unharmed. He had shot down one of the Zeros (probably the one that had got the big burst in on us) and the other decided to call it quits."

He concluded, "We found that our plane had been hit 55 times."

You can read the rest of McClusky's interview here: www.cv6.org/company/accounts/wmcclusky

BOOKS

The Empire Falls: The Battle of Midway by Steve White

Midway 1942: Turning Point in the Pacific by Mark Stille

Unbroken by Laura Hillenbrandt

INTERNET

There's a lot of great information on the Battle of Midway at a website maintained by Naval History & Heritage Command. Check out links to historical footage of the battle and profiles of Midway's leaders: www.history.navy.mil/browse-by-topic/wars-conflicts-and-operations/world-war-ii/1942/midway.html

MOVIES

The Battle of Midway (1942). This film uses footage by US naval cameramen in the Battle of Midway. Directed by John Ford, this documentary is a stirring reminder of combat sacrifice.

THE TWO BATTLES OF ATTU

1942 and 1943

Japanese soldiers on Attu Island, Alaska 1942. Notice the fog on the mountainsides.

REMEMBER HOW ADMIRAL Yamamoto's plan for the attack on Midway involved two operations? Operation MI didn't work out too well for the Japanese.

But Operation AL was a different story. Yamamoto's plan allowed enemy forces to get on American soil in Alaska's Aleutian Islands.

In 1942, Alaska and Hawaii weren't states—both were American territories. Both Alaska and Hawaii also had significant military bases, due to their strategic locations. Alaska alone had more than 42,000 American servicemen.

"...whoever holds Alaska will hold the world," said General Billy Mitchell, testifying before Congress in 1935. "I think it is the most strategic place in the world."

Japan thought so, too.

Look at the map below. Alaska is gigantic—twice as big as Texas with more coastline than the entire United States combined. Its Aleutian Islands stretch more than 1,000 miles across the northern Pacific Ocean. The islands almost touch Russia and Japan is just to their south.

Map of Alaska, with the Aleutian Islands stretching toward the Soviet Union

Dutch Harbor was the main American naval base in the Aleutians (see map). It held about 15,000 American troops. Does that sound like a lot? Maybe not, if you consider how much land and sea needed protection.

Since Americans cracked the Japanese secret code, Admiral Nimitz knew that Yamamoto planned to attack the Aleutians. So Nimitz ordered Task Force 8 to leave Pearl Harbor in May. Five cruisers, fourteen destroyers, and six submarines all set sail for Alaska. Their commander, Rear Admiral Robert Theobald, was ordered to protect the naval facility at Dutch Harbor—at all costs.

In early June, while the Battle of Midway was taking place, a Japanese carrier force attacked Dutch Harbor.

Of course, Yamamoto expected America to divert its carriers away from Midway and head to Alaska. But he didn't know the Americans were one step ahead of him. Cracking that Japanese code allowed the Americans to hold onto Dutch Harbor.

Only it wasn't a victory. Thousands of Japanese troops managed to land on other Aleutian Islands—Agattu, Kiska, and Attu (see map).

That meant that for the first time since the War of 1812, when the British invaded, enemy forces occupied part of America.

Japan planted its red-and-white flag in American soil.

The occupation was a serious problem for the United States. Japan could interrupt shipping routes that ran across the northern Pacific that were used to send aid to the Soviet Union, which was an American ally during WWII. Military leaders also worried that the Japanese would move from the islands into mainland Alaska. From there, they could invade the western states of Washington, Oregon, and California.

America would have liked to take immediate action against the occupying Japanese. But it was already fighting two fronts in this war: in the southern Pacific against Japan and in Europe against Germany and Italy.

It didn't have enough troops or supplies to start yet another fight in Alaska.

So for an entire year, thousands of Japanese troops stayed

on Attu and Kiska.

Finally, when the war against Germany and Italy seemed under control in North Africa, the American military sent those troops to Alaska to remove the Japanese.

Code named Operation Sandcrab, the invasion of Attu Island was such a top secret mission that not even the soldiers chosen for the attack knew where they were going. Since most of these men were coming from the battlefields of North Africa, they assumed the military was sending them to another hot climate. After all, they saw orders for lots of mosquito netting.

The trouble began even before the troops left San Francisco. Cargo ships carrying their supplies and military material were so small that many essential items—like winter clothing—were left behind. Since Operation Sandcrab was taking place during the summer, the military didn't think these men would need warm clothes. Plus, they expected the invasion to last only about thirty-six hours.

But summer in Alaska isn't like summer in California.

Soldiers unload landing craft on the beach at Attu

The troops left San Francisco with only lightweight uniforms. Heading north, still uncertain of their destination, the men watched as ice formed on the ship rails. A nonstop wind was so cold that it blew right through their cotton clothing. Despite the calendar saying it was summer, the mountains were still covered with snow. The valleys were cold, wet, and boggy.

On May 11, 1943, the invasion of Attu began.

The garrison of 2,300 Japanese soldiers didn't fight back against the initial assault. If they had, the invasion might have ended right there. Not only did the American troops have the wrong clothing, they also had inaccurate maps. So they landed in the wrong locations, only to discover they didn't have enough of the right equipment. Landing vehicles got stuck on the beaches or sank into the marshy Alaska soil called muskeg.

Cold and desolate, these volcanic islands were nothing like the sandy deserts of North Africa.

Soon soldiers were suffering from frostbite and trench foot as they trudged over snowy cliffs. Their thin leather boots stayed wet, day and night.

And then, the Japanese attacked.

Hidden on the ridges, the Japanese soldiers opened fire with machine guns and mortars. Other times, the combat became so close that it was hand-to-hand. But even when the American artillery set up on Attu's beaches, it was hard to locate the enemy. The island stayed cloaked in a dense fog, hiding positions.

Wearing their thin uniforms and sleeping in canvas tents, the Americans scoured the island for the Japanese soldiers who wore fur-lined coats and kept small kerosene stoves for heat. The American soldiers became so cold they burned their rifle stocks to get warm.

Yet, they kept fighting.

Within two weeks, the Americans had inflicted serious damage on the Japanese forces. And finally, the military was sending reinforcements and proper equipment to Attu.

On the evening of May 28, right before the supplies were to arrive, a reconnaissance patrol crept up to one of the Japanese encampments. What they saw was very strange. The Japanese soldiers were guzzling sake—Japanese rice wine—and yelling at the top of their lungs.

American troops hauling supplies on Attu because their vehicles couldn't travel over the island's rugged terrain. May 1943.

Nearby, their wounded comrades were committing suicide with self-inflicted gunshots.

The Americans crawled away, confused.

What they didn't know was that Japan's new military leaders had spread propaganda among the people. Manipulating the Bushido code, leaders convinced the soldiers that dying for one's country wasn't just a duty, it was a "holy mission." They told them that wounded men only slowed down the mission. Plus they said the Americans were evil and did terrible things to soldiers. Japanese men were better off committing suicide than being captured.

That strange behavior seen by the Americans on Attu was actually preparation for a suicide mission, known as a Banzai attack.

Early the next morning, Japanese soldiers crept silently through Attu's heavy fog. Several American infantry units were just beginning to eat breakfast when they heard blood-curdling screams.

"Banzai!"

The Japanese soldiers raced out of the fog, overpowered three sentry outposts, and took an American field hospital. Under the Geneva Convention, all medical tents were marked with the red-and-white symbol of the International Red Cross, indicating a no-fighting zone.

Running through the field hospital, Japanese soldiers bayonetted unarmed medical personnel and slashed the wounded laying helplessly on their cots. The sound of gunfire alerted the 50th Combat Engineers. They were on a hill above the hospital. Grabbing their M-1 rifles and helmets, the engineers lined up along the hill's crest, only to see Japanese soldiers charging toward them, bayonets aimed to murder. The engineers only managed to fire off one or two rounds before the enemy was on them in hand-to-hand combat. Using rifle butts and fists, the outnumbered engineers beat back the Japanese troops, who once again disappeared into the fog.

And that was how the Americans learned about Banzai attacks.

The next time they heard the enemy screaming, they were

ready. Once again, they beat back the Japanese soldiers.

Three days later, the Americans had fought to gain the upper hand.

On May 31, the Americans finally defeated the Japanese.

All 3,000 Japanese soldiers on Attu were dead.

But American forces paid a high price for this victory, suffering almost 4,000 casualties, many from the cold and disease, and 549 men were killed in action.

When Attu was cleared of the enemy, the Americans headed for the next Aleutian objective—Kiska.

Nearly 5,000 Japanese soldiers were on that island.

But on August 15, when the Americans landed on Kiska, the Japanese garrison was gone.

All that remained were four dogs.

And the corpse of one Japanese soldier.

WHO FOUGHT?

A group of approximately 40 dead Japanese soldiers at a ridge on Attu, Aleutian
Islands, US Territory of Alaska, May 29, 1943

"MODERN ARMIES HAD never fought before in any field that was like the Aleutians," said Dashiell Hammett, a US Army corporal. Hammett spent eighteen months on the Aleutian Island of Adak. Later, he became a famous mystery novelist. But his time in the Aleutians left a deep impression. "We could borrow no knowledge from the past. We would have to learn as we went along, how to live and fight and win in this land, the least-known part of America."

The learning curve was steep. But among the quickest students were the US Army Combat Engineers.

With the fighting going on around them, the engineers had to figure out how to keep food, water, and ammunition moving, even when the trucks and tractors were bogged down in the muskeg. Realizing their military equipment was almost useless, the engineers used streams and waterways as roads. Soon, artillery and ammunition were floating to various locations. When the terrain grew steep, the engineers built a cable system to haul everything from backpacks to wooden carts onto higher ground. They also created a supply hub on a hill overlooking a wide valley. They figured that from that location, their artillery could shell the Japanese who were dug into even higher ground.

That rise was later named "Engineer Hill."

It was also where the army engineers faced that Banzai attack.

BOOKS

Ghosts in the Fog: The Untold Story of Alaska's WWII Invasion by
   Samantha Seiple

*The Capture of Attu: A World War II Battle as Told by the Men Who
   Fought There* by Gregory J.W. Urwin

First Among Men: A Story of the Invasion of Attu Island by Jerry Coke

INTERNET

Check out this 1940s newsreel about the Battle of Attu:
youtube.com/watch?v=jtFkIBrFcQo

MOVIES

Red, White, Black & Blue. Critically acclaimed documentary about the Battle of Attu with interviews of veterans from the invasion campaign.

THE PT BOAT

Early PT boat. Notice the two torpedoes on this side and the twin .50-caliber machine guns.

YOU MIGHT THINK torpedoes are a new invention. But as far back as 1275, an inventor was thinking about "an egg which moves itself and burns."

The torpedo as we know it appeared in the late 1800s. Earlier torpedoes operated more like underwater mines that exploded when touched. But a British engineer named Robert Whitehead figured out how to propel those explosive mines through the water, creating the modern torpedo.

Unfortunately, Whitehead's early torpedoes were slow and unreliable. They couldn't be counted on to hit their target.

Whitehead kept working on his invention. By 1870 he had figured out how to use compressed air with an explosive charge to fire the torpedo, pushing it through the water as far as 1,000 yards. Still, these torpedoes weren't fast enough. Sometimes they didn't stay underwater.

Whitehead refused to quit.

By 1881, his torpedo design was so good that ten countries ordered it for their navies. Other inventors tinkered with the invention, improving its speed and accuracy. By 1900, the torpedo was considered a worthy weapon for warfare. It was sinking ships.

The next decision was to determine what kind of ship should be used for firing the torpedoes.

In the early 1900s, huge battleships ruled the seas, but they were expensive to build. For the same cost as one battleship, a country could build dozens of smaller boats that could fire torpedoes and do some serious damage in battle.

But, just like the torpedo itself, the torpedo boat took a while to perfect.

The first boats were manufactured in the United States. They were called PT boats, for Patrol Torpedo. Early models were sold to other countries because America's military didn't think they were good enough. The Navy continued to demand massive destroyers instead.

In the 1930s, America suddenly had interests in the Philippine Islands. These patrol boats were useful for coastal defenses. Several boat builders competed to win a military contract. Each patrol boat entry was numbered from *PT-1* through *PT-19*. The Navy tested them all, but once again decided the PT wasn't up to American military standards.

In 1941, the Electric Boat Company (Elco) designed the *PT-*

20.

Seventy-seven feet long, weighing thirty-three tons, PT-20 carried four torpedoes, eight depth charges, and two dual .50 caliber machine guns. It had three engines boosting the wooden vessel to speeds of 41 knots or 47 miles per hour (one knot is equal to 1.15 mph).

That same year, Japan bombed Pearl Harbor. Suddenly the PT boat looked even better.

PT crews consisted of two officers and ten enlisted men. As WWII progressed, the PT boats started carrying smaller—but more powerful—torpedoes. Sometimes they had radar. Quick-moving and deadly, the PT boats attacked cruisers, destroyers, submarines, and supply barges. They were used everywhere from the South Pacific and the Aleutian Islands to the Mediterranean Sea and the English Channel.

These "buccaneers of the sea" destroyed hundreds of barges loaded with Japanese troops and supplies. PT boats also snuck into enemy harbors, conducted sabotage, and went on raiding missions behind enemy lines. They also rescued Allied crews whose planes went down at sea.

Fighting against massive coastal guns and ships 100 times their size—and winning—the PT boats were soon known as "the mosquito fleet."

The Japanese, however, after suffering many losses because of them, called the PTs "Devil Boats."

WHO FOUGHT?

PT 109 in the South Pacific

ON THE MOONLESS night of August 2, 1943, Lieutenant John F. Kennedy and his crew aboard *PT-109* were idling quietly on one engine, trying to avoid Japanese detection.

But around 2:00 a.m., the crew suddenly realized that a Japanese destroyer was headed straight toward them. With only ten seconds to fire up the engines, *PT-109* was sliced in half by the destroyer. The collision killed two men and badly injured two others. The only thing keeping the boat afloat were its watertight compartments in the forward hull. The rest of the boat was in flames.

Eleven survivors clung to the bow as it drifted slowly south. When the hull started taking on water, Kennedy decided the crew's best chance of survival was to swim for some nearby islands. However, Kennedy knew the larger islands contained Japanese prison camps.

Placing the men who couldn't swim on a piece of wood that was once the boat's gun mount, Kennedy and his men swam for a smaller island. An expert swimmer, Kennedy clenched the strap of one man's life vest between his teeth, carrying the man more than three miles until they reached shore.

The island was only 100 yards across—the size of a football field. It had no food or fresh water. And the crew needed to hide from passing Japanese barges. Kennedy swam another two-and-a-half miles in search of food and help. Then he led his men to another island that had fresh water and coconut trees.

Kennedy and the ten surviving men lived on coconuts and rainwater until some island natives discovered them and offered shelter. Each night, Kennedy would send out signals, hoping to make contact with one of the American naval ships in the area.

Six days later, a patrol boat came to their rescue.

Kennedy was later awarded military honors for his courage and leadership under fire.

In 1960, he became the 35th president of the United States.

BOOKS

PT Boats in Action—Warships No. 34 by David Doyle

John F. Kennedy and PT-109 by Richard Tregaskis

ELCO 80 PT Boat—On Deck Color Series No. 5 by David Doyle

Higgins PT Boats On Deck by David Doyle

INTERNET

Here's a YouTube video of the only operational PT boat still in existence: youtube.com/watch?v=ucciZ1zFpXY

Longer video on the history and use of the PT during WWII: youtube.com/watch?v=FtMJFROT2zk

MOVIES

They Were Expendable

PT 109

GUADALCANAL

August 7, 1942 – February 9, 1943

Japanese soldier throwing a grenade on Guadalcanal

WITH THE SURPRISE of the Doolittle Raid and the victory at Midway, morale was rising among the Allied forces in the Pacific.

But Japan was still winning the war.

Island after island, the Japanese forces steamrolled through the South Pacific. Japan would soon control enough territory to dominate the entire region.

The American military decided the best way to fight back

was to pick certain islands that needed to be kept out of Japanese hands. One of the most crucial islands was Guadalcanal.

Located in the larger chain of Solomon Islands, some 2,000 miles north of Australia, Guadalcanal is ninety miles long, twenty-five miles wide, and covered by tropical jungles. It was big enough for an airfield.

In 1942, Japanese troops had already landed on the neighboring island of Tulaghi (pronounced "two-log-ee"). If the Japanese also took Guadalcanal, they would be able to cut off the sea route that linked Australia to the United States. Plus the Japanese Air Force could launch strikes on the West—just as Midway Island would have allowed American forces to attack Japan. Lastly, Guadalcanal would give Japan an even bigger defensive buffer zone around its mainland islands.

In early 1942, Admiral Ernest King had presented a plan to block Japan from building land and air bases in the Solomon Islands. But the Navy turned it down due to costs and manpower shortages. At that point, the war in Europe was taking first priority.

But priorities changed in July when the military learned that Japan had already sent a 3,000-man construction battalion to Guadalcanal.

The fight was on to take Guadalcanal.

But to win, America needed its toughest men. Men who could fight on both land and sea. Men who wouldn't back down, no matter what the enemy threw at them.

Who were these men? The marines.

The marines who fought on Guadalcanal were so tough that the Japanese called them "gangsters" and "thugs."

Marines landing on Guadalcanal

THE PLAN

ADMIRAL KING'S PLAN to take Guadalcanal seemed straightforward enough. The 1st and 5th Marine Divisions would sail for the island, secure a beachhead, then assist other American landing forces.

Reality proved more complicated.

The marines were young. Many of them were barely out of high school. They had enlisted right after the attack on Pearl Harbor, and most of them had no combat experience. The Navy had assured their commander, Major General Alexander Vandegrift, that these boys would be trained once they reached the Pacific.

Unfortunately, more than half of the divisions reached Guadalcanal right before the landing invasion.

There were other problems, too. The naval force carrying the marines didn't have much experience with amphibious— land and sea—missions. They also lacked the most essential field supplies such as accurate maps, tidal charts, and information about the underwater hazards near the beaches. In order to get that information, the marines resorted to reading old National Geographic magazines and German nautical charts from World War I.

On August 7, 1942, ten thousand marines reached Guadalcanal, supported by the most powerful amphibious force ever assembled—three carriers, one battleship, five cruisers, and twenty-four support ships.

Why so much support?

Because they expected the Japanese to fight this landing to the death.

But oddly, when the marines headed for the beaches, they found almost no opposition.

That would be the last time anything seemed easy on Guadalcanal.

Back in Tokyo, Japanese officials heard about the American landing. They dispatched a naval force that arrived two days later at nearby Savo Island. Japan struck the task force so fiercely that America pulled every one of its ships from the area. It was only seven months after Pearl Harbor, and America couldn't afford to lose any more ships or troops.

The Japanese forces scooped up almost all of the marine's supplies. Food, fresh water, ammunition. Barbed wire. Antipersonnel mines. Everything needed to survive on Guadalcanal.

Japan controlled the water around island, so the American marines were surrounded.

Yet despite their dire circumstances, the marines pushed across the island to the Japanese-built airfield. They drove out the enemy forces.

So Japan bombed the runway.

The marines repaired it—using equipment the Japanese left

behind.

In late August, nineteen Wildcat fighters and twelve Dauntless dive bombers managed to land at the newly-named Henderson Field, named for Lofton Henderson, a marine pilot killed during the Battle of Midway.

But conditions were much worse. The tropical jungles bred mosquitoes that carried malaria. Nearly every marine on Guadalcanal suffered from the disease's symptoms—fevers, chills, headaches, vomiting. Guadalcanal's other dangers included enormous poisonous spiders and crabs that crawled up the sand from the sea and bit people. Deadly crocodiles slithered through the swampy water, eager to devour any living creature.

US Marine patrol crosses the Matanikau River on Guadalcanal, September, 1942

Then the heavy tropical rains arrived. The marines slept in foxholes full of water. The constant damp conditions rotted away their boots. With no supplies to replace the boots, men were forced to fight barefoot.

The marines also received reinforcements, boosting their numbers to about 23,000. Soon, the food shortages became so chronic that the marines were eating leaves and bugs. When they captured a Japanese encampment, the marines celebrated because the camp included barrels of fish heads and rice. But as the starving marines dove into the food, they realized it was moving. Worms! They ate it anyway.

Young and inexperienced, the marines fighting their way across Guadalcanal learned about Japanese tactics the hard way. At one point, some island natives approached the Americans. They said some Japanese troops were ready to surrender. So twenty-five marines got in boats and paddled to where the Japanese soldiers stood, waving a white flag. Only three marines returned. That "surrender" was an ambush. One of the captured marines was used for Japanese bayonet practice—while still alive.

The marines kept up constant patrols. Attacks were usually hand-to-hand combat using knives, logs, shovels, or anything they could find.

General Vandegrift would later say, "There were a hundred reasons why this operation should fail."

But sick, barefoot, starving, and exhausted, the Guadalcanal marines fought more than a dozen significant battles over the course of six months. To describe them all here would take a very long time. But here are some of the most important battles.

Marine on Guadalcanal

August 9, 1942: Naval Battle of Savo Island

The Japanese navy forced the American navy to retreat, leaving the marines alone on Guadalcanal short of supplies and ammunition.

August 21: Naval Battle of Tenaru

During the night, Japanese Colonel Kiyonao Ichiki and 800 of his men attacked a perimeter held by America's 2nd Battalion. The Japanese hoped to destroy the Henderson Field airstrip.

They first killed an American gunner with a bullet to the head, then wounded the gun commander. Shredding the water jacket of a machine gun, the Japanese lobbed a grenade into the machine gun pit.

That explosion blinded marine Al Schmid. But Schmid kept firing. Since Schmid couldn't see, his wounded gun commander had to tap Schmid's arm to tell him where to aim. By the next morning, the two marines were still alive. But more than 200 Japanese soldiers were dead in front of them. Schmid was later awarded the Navy Cross, along with the gun commander and the dead gunner.

September 12–14: Battle of the Ridge

When the Americans took Henderson Airfield, they formed a defensive perimeter. But one side was bordered by the Pacific Ocean. Commander Vandegrift suspected the Japanese would attack from there. Sure enough, on September 12, Japanese bombers struck the airfield from the ocean. Later that night, Japanese destroyers and a cruiser shelled the same area, followed by the Japanese infantry attacking from land. But those Japanese infantry troops were exhausted.

They had been marching through Guadalcanal's thick jungle. The tropical humidity had ruined their communications equipment, too. Their assault failed.

The following day, the Japanese renewed their attack. Two thousand soldiers struck the American lines but were confronted by marine machine guns and artillery fire. By the next night, this battle had killed or wounded many men on both sides: 448 marines and paramarines (marine paratroopers), and 1,200 Japanese soldiers.

Officials in Tokyo realized these Americans were not going to stop fighting for Guadalcanal. So they sent more resources to the island, including another 20,000 Japanese troops.

The marines also received reinforcements, boosting their numbers to about 23,000. However, one-third of these men were unable to fight because of various sicknesses and diseases, including dysentery, a painful intestinal infection caused by the waterborne bacteria and parasites. Since the Japanese troops had been fighting in this area, their immune systems protected them from the sicknesses.

October 13–14: Henderson Field

Two Japanese battleships fired more than 700 fourteen-inch

shells. Each shell contained 600 steel cylinders filled with magnesium and barium nitrate. When detonated, these incendiaries burn at 3,000 degrees. The shelling against the Americans continued all night. The marines refuse to surrender.

October 22–25: Japanese Counteroffensive

Some 5,000 Japanese soldiers attacked the American positions around Henderson Airfield, while another 7,000 soldiers concentrated to the south. Several Japanese troops manage to breach the American defensive perimeter, but the marines drove them back. The Japanese lost 3,500 men.

October 26–27: Naval Battle of Santa Cruz Island

As the battles continued and the marines refused to back down, Japanese forces fell into disarray. Vandegrift decided it was time to fight offensively, rather than defensively guarding American positions. But the marines who landed there in August were ravaged from months of jungle fighting. In November, the 1st Marine Division was replaced by the 25th Infantry Division and the 2nd Marine Division.

Japanese officials in Tokyo also sent more troops to Guadalcanal.

November 12–15: Naval Battle of Guadalcanal

Eleven Japanese transport ships arrived with reinforcements. American pilots sank six ships, damaged another, and forced four ships to be beached. Only 2,000 Japanese troops reached the island. Most of their equipment was lost at sea.

December 17: General Patch's Offensives

The marine offensive was so powerful that the Emperor of

Japan decided to withdraw forces.

By February 1943, all the enemy forces had left Guadalcanal.

Not only did this victory boost morale among the troops, America now controlled an important airfield complex in the South Pacific. It also had a valuable anchorage to secure sea routes to Australia and protect the Aussies from a Japanese invasion.

But the victory also cost many lives on both sides.

Some 14,000 Japanese troops were killed at Guadalcanal. Another 9,000 men died of diseases. Japan also lost 26 naval ships, 600 airplanes, and 6 submarines.

About 1,600 American soldiers were killed in action at Guadalcanal. Thousands more died of tropical diseases. Another 4,300 were wounded. America also lost eight cruisers, two heavy carriers, and fourteen destroyers.

So many ships were lost on both sides that a channel north of Guadalcanal was nicknamed "Iron Bottom Sound."

WHO FOUGHT?

John Basilone, wearing his Medal of Honor

THE MARINES AND paramarines who fought at Guadalcanal were among the finest soldiers America has ever produced, including Marine Sgt. John Basilone. When Japanese grenades and mortar fire reduced his fifteen-man unit to two, Basilone moved an extra gun into position, manning it himself while he repaired the damaged gun. Almost single-handedly, Basilone held the line until replacements arrived. When the Japanese cut off the supply lines and ammunition was running low, Basilone fought his way—once again under continual fire—through enemy lines to bring shells to his gunners.

When the smoke cleared, Basilone's platoon had stopped an entire Japanese regiment. More than 300 enemy soldiers lay dead.

Basilone was awarded the Congressional Medal of Honor.

Later, he would also receive the Navy Cross, the only enlisted marine to receive both medals during World War II.

BOOKS

Guadalcanal Diary by Richard Tregaskis

Fight to the Death by Larry Hama

The Battle of Guadalcanal: Land and Sea Warfare in the South Pacific by Larry Hama and Anthony Williams

Hero of the Pacific by James Brady. Esteemed author's biography of Marine John Basilone.

I'm Staying With My Boys: The Heroic Life of Sgt. John Basilone USMC by Jim Proser, Jerry Cutter. Family-authorized biography.

The Ghosts of Iron Bottom Sound by Sandy Nelson. A New Zealand schoolboy becomes obsessed with the wrecks of warships sunk in the battles at Guadalcanal.

INTERNET

Probably the finest collection of online information about Guadalcanal comes from the National WWII Museum. The site offers some interesting activities online from making your own WWII-era armed services patch to teaching you how to send messages with navy flags. www.nationalww2museum.org/see-hear/kids-corner.html

You can read about each Medal of Honor soldier from Guadalcanal here: www.worldwar2history.info/II/Medal-of-Honor/Guadalcanal.html

MOVIES

Guadalcanal Diary

The Galant Hours

Pride of the Marines (the story of Al Schmidt)

TARAWA

November 20 − 23, 1943

The LVT, or Landing Vehicle Tracked, heading into The Battle of Tarawa

OCEANS MOVE IN a definite pattern. High tide raises the water level on shore. Low tide takes the water back out, leaving behind the bare beach. These tides are controlled by gravitational forces between the sun and moon.

But twice a month, on the moon's first and third quarter, something unusual happens. The gravitational forces between the sun and moon cancel each other out. That means there's almost no difference between high and low tide, because there's no strong pull between the sun and moon.

This phenomena is called a neap tide.

One of the Pacific's fiercest battles was affected by a neap tide. In fact, you might even say that a neap tide was responsible for the deaths of many American soldiers.

It happened on Tarawa Island.

Another tiny atoll in the South Pacific, Tarawa is linked with a smaller island named Betio. This island is half the size of Central Park in New York City.

Japan had transformed this speck on the sea into one of the most heavily-fortified islands in the Pacific. Japanese soldiers dug hundreds of concrete bunkers, called pillboxes, into the ground. These were used to store weapons and to protect soldiers from bombs or other attacks. The Japanese also erected seawalls which were difficult for men to climb over and created trenches that connected all points of the island. This setup allowed more than 4,500 Japanese troops stationed at Betio to move anywhere underground. They tore out trees and created an airstrip down the middle of the island.

All of this was protected with coastal guns, anti-aircraft guns, heavy and light machine guns, and light tanks.

Japan was so proud of this fortification that Admiral Keiji Shibazaki bragged that "it would take a million men one hundred years" to conquer Tarawa.

The marines would put that boast to the test. America's military leaders had devised a strategy called "island hopping." They picked select islands for bases that could bring American troops closer to Japan as well as isolated or contained other islands with naval or air power. The goal was to reach Japan.

The Tarawa atoll lay in the path of this advance on Japan.

But in addition to all those Japanese fortifications, Tarawa was surrounded by dangerous coral reefs. Even the toughest amphibious vehicles couldn't get across these mineral embankments. So the military brought in LVTs—Landing Vehicle Tracked. These machines are sometimes called Amtracks or even Alligators. Used experimentally elsewhere, such as in the battles in North Africa, these machines worked much like amphibious tanks, crawling out of the water onto land. They also came equipped with machine guns. Each LVT could carry twenty troops. The Navy sent to Tarawa the largest American invasion force yet assembled for one Pacific operation: seventeen aircraft carriers, twelve battleships, eight heavy cruisers, four light cruisers, sixty-six destroyers, and thirty-six transport ships carrying 35,000 troops from the 2nd Marine Division and part of the Army's 27th Infantry Division.

The marines would land on three beachheads named Red 1, Red 2, and Red 3.

Japanese Admiral Shibazaki ordered his Imperial Marines—the strongest men—to defend the island.

At 5:10 a.m. on November 20, the American battleships, cruisers, and destroyers opened fire on Tarawa. After thirty minutes of shelling from the water, the pilots flew out, inflicting a seven-minute air strike. Then the ships opened fire again—this time for two-and-a-half hours.

"Fires were burning everywhere," Captain Charles Moore later said. "The coconut trees were blasted and burned and it seemed that no living soul could be on the island…the troops approached the beach and it looked like the whole affair would be a walkover."

Other naval officers were just as confident. They said the marines would walk in "standing up," not crouching under enemy fire.

Some 100 LVTs headed for the beachhead. Suddenly deadly

gunfire filled the air.

The American bombardment hadn't damaged the Japanese military fortifications enough.

"The bullets were pouring at us like sheet rain," one marine recalled. "We were one hundred yards in now and the enemy fire was awful damn intense and getting worse. They were knocking boats out left and right. A tractor'd get hit, stop, and burst into flames, with men jumping out like torches."

The LVTs climbed over the coral. Some shallow-bottomed boats followed, sent out at high tide to clear the gnarly reefs.

But there was no high tide. It was a neap tide.

The boats got stuck on the reefs, leaving the troops easy targets for the Japanese already shooting holes in the LVTs. If an LVT reached the beach, it still couldn't clear the seawall. Men were pinned against the logs. The LVT drivers, realizing the boats were stuck on the reefs, headed back out to rescue them, even as bullets zipped past their heads. Other men climbed out of the boats and staggered for the beach.

"It was painfully slow, wading in such deep water," recalled war correspondent Robert Sherrod. "And we had seven hundred yards to walk slowly into that machine-gun fire, looming into larger targets as we rose onto higher ground. I was scared, as I had never been scared before. But my head was clear. I was extremely alert, as though my brain were dictating that I live these last minutes for all they were worth."

The Japanese wiped out half the LVTs that day. On the beach, dead and wounded Americans covered the sand.

The enemy gunfire didn't stop. Some marines stayed behind the seawall. Marines landing at Red 3 used long piers for cover, but communication was stopped when salt water damaged their radios.

American Marines advancing from behind a Tarawa sea wall

After ninety minutes of relentless shooting, Colonel David M. Shoup, senior officer of the landing forces, managed to call in an "All possible fire support." Though wounded by an exploding shell, Shoup managed to clear the pier of Japanese snipers.

Over the next two days, under constant enemy fire, Shoup led several attacks against the Japanese, pushing the marines forward. For his heroic actions on Betio, Shoup would be awarded the Medal of Honor. By dusk of the first day, the Japanese had destroyed American tanks, bulldozers, and severely limited what medical supplies could reach shore.

The sand turned red from blood.

But the marines managed to hold about 1,000 yards of beach.

On the second day, the neap tide continued, so the next wave of landings experienced the same problems. Struggling ashore in chest-high water, bullets ripping the water around them, the troops that reached the shore found low supplies of ammunition, food, and fresh water.

The beach continued to pile up with dead and wounded men. Wrecked equipment twisted in the barbed wire traps.

Without tanks and artillery, the marines had little chance of destroying the enemy's concrete bunkers and pillboxes. However, toward the end of the second day, the neap tide faded. The ocean began to rise. At high tide, five destroyers pushed close enough to blast the pillboxes, and the landing craft were able to carry desperately needed tanks and artillery to the beach.

Using flamethrowers, the American tanks burned a path forward into the island, blowing up the pillboxes one by one.

For both sides, the battle was a take-no-prisoners fight.

On the third day, the marines approached a massive bunker. Inside were Admiral Shibazaki and 300 of his remaining men.

Bulldozers piled the sand high against the bunker's entrances. Then the marines poured gasoline into the bunker, and topped it off with a hand grenade.

When it exploded, the battle of Tarawa was over. The Americans had won.

However, this battle is distinctly remembered for the highest loss of life in the first seventy-five hours of any Pacific battle. During those three days, more than 1,300 marines were killed. An entire 4,500-man Japanese garrison was wiped out.

After learning hard lessons from the botched landings at Tarawa, Admiral Nimitz ordered replicas made of Japanese fortifications. The models were built on outlying Hawaiian islands so the military could practice how to destroy them.

The experiences at Tarawa also led to the development of

waterproofed radios and a stronger focus on natural phenomena, such as the mystery of tides.

WHO FOUGHT?

IN *ONE SQUARE Mile of Hell: The Battle of Tarawa*, author John Wukovits described how battlefield fighting affects human behavior.

"Lt. Frank Plant, Jr. concluded that three categories of men existed in battle. Some froze and could do nothing to contribute. For instance he unsuccessfully tried to halt one terrorized private who dug deeper and deeper into the sand, as if in doing so he could escape the carnage. Not far from this private, two other marines, rigid with fear, lay immobile on the ground with their arms extended at right angles. "The other extreme offered those, like Hawkins, who not only ignored every risk but seemed eager to face them. He called them 'sons of guns' who inspired the men, and concluded 'Most of them probably lost their lives.'

" 'The vast majority,' he decided, 'stood in the middle of the two extremes, following orders and killing Japanese because that was what they were supposed to do.' "

These young men faced a powerful and well-fortified enemy. Though it was inevitable that many of them would die, they courageously chose to fight. And because they didn't give up, they ultimately won.

BOOKS

World War II Battles and Leaders by DK Publishing (2004)

Tarawa 1943: The Turning of the Tide by Derrick Wright

Marines in World War II—The Battle for Tarawa by Captain James R. Stockman U.S.M.C.

INTERNET

Eyewitness to History offers some more information about the Battle of Tarawa: www.eyewitnesstohistory.com/tarawa.htm

MOVIES

War in Tarawa. Documentary on the brutal Battle of Tarawa

THE BATTLE OF SAIPAN

June 15 – July 9, 1944

American marines take cover behind an M4 Sherman tank while clearing Japanese forces from the northern end of Saipan, July 8, 1944

THE COURAGEOUS FIGHTING by the American and Allied forces eventually captured large areas of the Pacific Ocean. The Solomon Islands, Gilbert Islands, Marshall Islands, and parts of New Guinea.

That's a lot of places.

But Japan still controlled even larger areas, including the Philippine Islands, the Caroline Islands, Palau Islands, and Mariana Islands. Look at the map below. It shows where these islands are located. Some are coral atolls. Others are volcanic outcroppings. But even "bumps in the water" allowed Japan to create defensive barriers around its homeland.

Japan also controlled the island of Saipan (pronounced "sigh-pan"). Look at the map below. Saipan is the first island marked among the Mariana Islands, north of the Philippines.

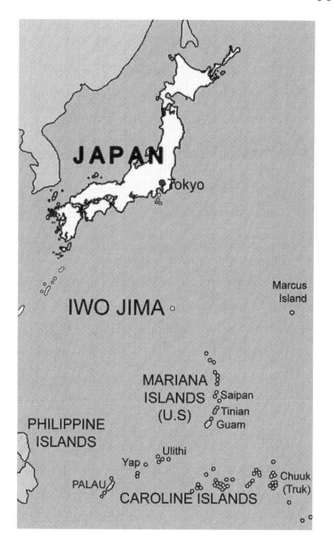

Though only seven miles across at its widest point and fifteen miles long, Saipan was big enough for the Japanese to build an airfield. For the Americans, it was close enough to

Japan that an attack could be launched on the Japanese homeland. It was especially advantageous since the Americans had a new long-range bomber—the Boeing B-29 Super Fortress. If America got control of Saipan, the Allies could disrupt Japanese supply lanes.

So both sides wanted Saipan.

But 30,000 Japanese troops were already on Saipan, under the command of Lt. General Yoshitsugu Saito.

The battle was on.

The American plan called for Lieutenant General Holland "Howlin Mad" Smith to attack Saipan with 127,000 men from the 2nd and 4th Marine divisions, along with the Army's 27th Division.

Americans would outnumber the Japanese three to one.

But the Japanese soldiers had one critical advantage—geography.

Saipan is a volcanic island. It has high cliffs and deep gullies. Dangerous coral reefs block every beach entrance except one on the eastern side.

Because there was just one coral-free beach, the Americans figured that Saito would expect them to land there. So they cleverly shifted the landing to Saipan's western side. The 2nd Marines took the northern beaches, while the 4th Marines took the island's southern end. They went everywhere *except* the eastern beach.

On June 13, 1944, fifteen American battleships fired 165,000 shells at Saipan. Another seven ships shot an additional 2,000 sixteen-inch shells. The attack continued for three days.

On June 15, with gunfire cover from the ships, the marines drove 300 LVTs over the coral reefs, carrying 8,000 men to the beaches.

Japanese soldiers were hidden in the cliffs above the beaches, armed with machine guns and artillery. The Japanese also had placed flags in the water so they could calculate range—which increased the killing rate—and destroyed twenty amphibious tanks. To further maximize American casualties, the Japanese had strung barbed wire across the island and dug hidden trenches.

The marines suffered some 2,000 casualties in one day.

But by nightfall, the 2nd and 4th divisions managed to establish a beachhead that was a half-mile deep and six miles across.

The Japanese then moved to wipe out the 4th Marines who landed to the south. Cunningly, Japanese soldiers had placed civilians in front of them, so the Americans only saw women and children approaching. They assumed it was a civilian surrender.

But the sneak attack backfired. The marines figured out the trick, took out the enemy, and preserved their own ranks.

Saito, meanwhile, was holding back most of his forces because he still expected the main attack to come from that coral-free beach on the eastern side.

On June 16, the Army's 27th Division landed—not on the coral-free beach—and joined up with other marines. Together, they captured the island's airfield.

Saito now realized his tactical error.

He ordered his first major attack on June 17. Under cover of darkness, he sent out forty-four light tanks for a night raid. But the American artillery destroyed three-quarters of the tanks. Worse for Saito, his attack had drawn the marines into new territory so they were in even better positions to attack the Japanese defenses.

The following day, Saito abandoned the attack and re-grouped his forces.

The marines kept pushing. They also helped secure two crucial areas, Nafutan Point, a short peninsula on the east coast, and Mount Nafutan, which was 400 feet high and gave the Americans high ground.

While the marines continued to attack the coastlines, General Smith ordered the army to move to the center of the island, effectively cutting the Japanese territory in half. Overhead, the Corsairs and Navy Hellcats bombarded the enemy positions.

However, the Japanese soldiers protected themselves by hiding in caves they dug into the volcanic cliffs. The island's geography hindered some of the American assaults. The worst fighting was in an area rightfully named Death Valley. The valley was south of the island's highest point, Mount Ta-potchau, which rose to a height of 1,500 feet. Another nearby cliff nearby was named Purple Heart Ridge. On those two lookout points, more than 10,000 Japanese troops were garrisoned. Whenever the Americans managed to thrash through the jungle forest, they came to the open valley, only to find Japanese firepower coming down at them from the high mounts.

The gunfire decimated the Americans.

But eventually, the Americans figured out how to clear the enemy from the caves using flamethrowers combined with cover fire from the artillery and machine guns.

Inch by inch, the Americans pressed forward.

But the Japanese had serious challenges, too. Their navy had recently suffered a crippling loss in the Philippine Sea. Their ships would not be coming with reinforcements or supplies for Saipan.

On June 27, the marines broke through Death Valley. Under heavy fire and casualties, they climbed the steep slopes of Mount Tapotchau and captured the island's highest point.

Now the Americans had a 1,500-foot lookout point and could track the enemy's movements.

By early July, the marines and army were marching toward the last section of Saipan still under Saito's control. Realizing the situation, Saito called Imperial Headquarters in Japan and asked permission for a "gyokusai," or Bansai suicide. He knew that he and his men were facing defeat.

Saito planned the suicide charge for July 7.

The night before, Saito gathered his soldiers. He ordered each of them to "take seven lives to repay our country."

Then Saito committed Hari Kari—suicide by stabbing a knife into his heart.

When the sun rose the next day, twelve soldiers carrying Japan's red-and-white flag led what remained of the Japanese forces, about 3,000 able-bodied men and thousands more limping behind them on crutches, their heads and limbs bandaged.

But it was enough to ambush the Americans.

The Banzai charge lasted twelve hours. It was the largest Banzai attack of the entire Pacific War.

One American who survived the attack, Major Edward McCarthy, described it like this:

"It reminded me of one of those old cattle-stampede scenes of the movies. The camera is in a hole in the ground, you see the herd coming, and they leap up and over you and are gone. Only the Japanese just kept coming and coming. I didn't think they'd ever stop."

The suicide charge killed or wounded hundreds of Americans.

But it also destroyed what remained of the Japanese troops. Thirty thousand of them were dead—most from fighting, some by suicide.

Tragically, in the final days of the battle, the Japanese government told their civilians that the Americans were barbarians, even cannibals, who would treat them cruelly. Rather than face capture, many of them climbed Saipan's high cliffs and leaped to their deaths.

Now that the Allies controlled Saipan, the American military was only 1,300 miles from the Japanese home islands. It wasn't long before some 100 American B-29 long-range bombers began landing on Saipan's airfield, preparing to attack Japan itself.

WHO FOUGHT?

Lt. Robert B. Sheeks served as an Intelligence and Japanese Language Officer. Here he speaks with a civilian woman and her children on Saipan, trying to persuade them to seek refuge. Sheeks' wartime experience is documented in the books *Pacific Legacy* and *One Marine's War*. This photograph was first published in *National Geographic* magazine, October 1944.

THE AMERICAN SOLDIERS on Saipan fought with valor and bravery, evidenced by the many medals won.

Here are some examples:

Under heavy fire, Lieutenant Colonel William J. O'Brien stood on the front lines with his men on Saipan, ordering them to hold the line. Armed with a .45 in each hand, O'Brien was badly wounded but refused to be evacuated because it might risk other men's lives. When the Japanese moved closer, O'Brien grabbed a rifle from another wounded soldier, climbed into a foxhole, and fired until he ran out of ammunition. He then spotted an abandoned jeep with a .50-caliber machine gun. He fired the gun until it also ran out of ammunition. The Japanese kept coming. The last his men saw of O'Brien, he was surrounded by saber-wielding Japanese. His last shouted words were, "Don't give them a damned inch!"

Sergeant Thomas A. Baker was also seriously wounded and also refused to leave his men, knowing that by carrying him to the rear, it would risk their lives. Instead, Baker asked them to place him against a pole, armed with a pistol containing eight bullets. Days after the battle, when Baker's body was found, eight Japanese soldiers lay dead around him.

Captain Ben L. Salomon was a surgeon with the 27th Infantry Division. He singlehandedly stopped seven Japanese soldiers who invaded his aid station. While his men evacuated about thirty wounded Americans, Salomon manned a machine gun post to cover their withdrawal. When Salomon's body was recovered after the battle, ninety-eight dead Japanese soldiers lay in front of his position. Salomon was posthumously awarded the Medal of Honor in 2002, the third Jewish service member to receive the medal for service in WWII.

BOOKS

Warriors in the Crossfire by Nancy Bo Flood. Set in WWII Saipan, this novel is highly rated by readers and reviewers. "An afterword describes the real-life account of what happened on Saipan, where almost all of the Japanese soldiers were killed, and duty-bound Japanese civilians were rounded up to take their own lives by jumping off what is now known as Suicide Cliff. Intense and powerful reading that avoids bleakness by celebrating family, culture, and a longing for peace. Grades 6–9."—*Booklist*, starred review.

INTERNET

History.com offers a concentrated source for digital footage on the Battle of Saipan: history.com/topics/world-war-ii/battle-of-saipan

For a detailed recounting of the fight for Mount Tapotchau, read this story from World War II magazine: www.historynet.com/mount-tapotchau-the-marines-take-saipans-high-ground.htm

MOVIES

Crusade in the Pacific: Battle for the Marianas. Part 15. Six Marine Corps cameramen were killed during the filming of this WWII documentary.

THE GREAT RAID

January 30, 1945

Company F, 6th Ranger Battalion, on patrol in the Philippines. No photos were taken of The Great Raid until it was over.

MANY OF THE American prisoners of war captured at Bataan and Corregidor were eventually shipped to a prison camp in the Philippines called Cabanatuan (pronounced "cuh-ban-nah-two-on").

It's hard to describe Cabanatuan. Not because we don't have details, but because the conditions were extremely terrible.

POWs were tortured, starved, and left to die from diseases.

Prisoners at Cabanatuan received two very small meals a day, usually just steamed rice with bugs in it. To survive, the POWs learned to bribe the guards for more food. They killed animals that wandered into the camp, such as mice and snakes. The Filipino underground smuggled in medicine, such as quinine, a crystalline compound made from tree bark used to treat malaria.

But maybe the most valuable item smuggled in was a radio.

Before they were captured, the POWs cleverly hid pieces of a radio inside their clothing. One piece of radio for each man. Once inside the camp, they reassembled the pieces and managed to find a broadcast signal. They heard news about the war outside the eight-foot barbed wire fences and armed guards. Some of the prisoners tried to escape from Cabanatuan. The majority didn't make it. When they were recaptured by the Japanese, they were beaten in front of the other prisoners, then forced to dig their own graves. The Japanese executed them, and the other prisoners were forced to bury them.

This psychological torture evolved into another rule. If any POW tried to escape, ten POWs would be shot. Then the guards placed the prisoners in groups of ten. Imagine being part of that group. Would you want anyone to try and escape? The Japanese knew this psychological torture would keep the POWs policing their own men.

Japan, however, was suffering as the war dragged on. It needed workers. So the stronger POWs were taken from Cabanatuan and sent to slave labor camps. They were forced to build weapons in Japanese factories—weapons used to kill their fellow Americans. The POWs also had to repair airfields so that Japanese bombers could go kill even more Americans.

The Geneva Convention banned this kind of abusive treatment of prisoners. But as you know, Japan signed the document but never followed its rules.

Cabanatuan originally held as many as 8,000 American and Filipino POWs, along with some captured civilians from Allied countries such as Great Britain and Norway. But with the slave labor camps growing rapidly, by 1944 there remained only about 500 POWs left at Cabanatuan.

These men were too sick for even slave labor.

With the battles of Tarawa and Saipan, Japan was no longer winning every fight. In early 1945, General Douglas MacArthur landed Allied forces on Luzon—the very same Philippine island where the Japanese had captured the POWs who were at Cabanatuan. MacArthur not only fulfilled his promise of "I shall return," but he was determined to retake the capital of Manila where 250,000 Japanese soldiers were waiting.

"Go around them, go through them, but go to Manila," MacArthur ordered.

Two days after the Luzon landing, an escaped POW named Eugene Nielsen came out of hiding. He told MacArthur's men a truly incredible story.

Nielsen said he and another 150 Americans had been forced to work as slave labor on a Japanese airfield. Every time the American Air Force bombed the field, the POWs had to fix it. They rose at dawn, received one small portion of maggot-infested rice, then worked to repair the damaged airfield until lunch. After more buggy rice, they worked until dark then were herded back to their compound.

This story was shocking to the American soldiers. Most of them had no idea about these horrific prison and slave labor camps.

But what Nielsen told them next was even more gruesome.

In early December, he and other POWs working the airfield were ordered back to the camp for lunch. But they were told to climb into their air raid shelters. The shelters were nothing more than slit trenches covered with logs. There was a small opening at each end.

Nielsen and the other prisoners climbed in—and smelled gasoline.

The Japanese guards had poured fuel into the shelter. On either end, they lit torches. Flames engulfed the trenches. The POWs crawled over each other as fire incinerated their bodies.

Miraculously, several men managed to escape.

Nielsen was one of them.

MacArthur's men took Nielsen to G-2, otherwise known as Army Intelligence.

Later it would be discovered that Japan had issued a "Kill All" order for the POWs. The enemy didn't want any of these prisoners testifying about how they were abused or else the Japanese soldiers would be tried for war crimes—and executed.

The Kill All policy read:

"Whether they are destroyed individually or in groups or however it is done, with mass bombing, poisonous smoke, poisons, drowning, decapitation, or what, dispose of them as the situation dictates. In any case it is the aim not to allow the escape of a single one, to annihilate them all, and not to leave any traces."

Nielsen's story was backed up by Major Robert Lapham. He, too, had escaped capture by the Japanese and was fighting as a guerrilla leader in the Philippines.

The last POWs at Cabanatuan, Philippines

On January 26, 1945, Lapham told the army about Cabanatuan. He said any remaining POWs at that camp were going to be killed—within days.

Those POW needed to be rescued. But how?

Even if the military could find the right soldiers for that mission, they'd have to train them in two days for a secret mission that was thirty miles away.

And who would lead them?

Lieutenant Colonel Henry Mucci was chosen.

Commander of the 6th Ranger Battalion, an elite group of warriors, Mucci had already trained his men in hand-to-hand combat, knife fighting, jungle survival, and marksmanship. Within hours, Mucci put together a POW rescue team with men from C Company and a platoon from F Company led by Captain Robert Prince.

Mucci told these men that they were going to raid Cabanatuan.

He also said there was a good chance they'd be killed.

But if they lived, "you're going to bring out every last man, even if you have to carry them on your backs."

"One other thing," Mucci added. "There'll be no atheists on this trip. I want you to swear an oath before God. Swear that you'll die fighting rather than let any harm come to those prisoners."

Mucci then took all his men to church.

Lt. Col. Henry Mucci

On the morning of January 28, the rangers headed out on trucks. They were taken to a secret drop-off location. After a short rest, they loaded two days' supplies into their packs, including a special surprise for the POWs—Hershey's chocolate bars.

In the early afternoon, they formed a column. Mucci was up front, and Captain Prince brought up the rear. As they crept through the Philippine jungle, they suddenly heard artillery shells flying past them. Then they realized that the fire power was coming from their own air force!

This rescue mission was so top secret, not even their fellow American soldiers knew about it.

The jungle foliage provided them cover but it also slowed their progress. In the rice paddies, thick mud sucked off their boots. The tropical heat sent sweat pouring down their faces.

Mucci didn't allow the men to carry anything that could reflect light. No rings or helmets. Only soft fatigue-colored hats that matched the rangers' faded clothing. But as elite rangers, these men could carry the weapon of their choice. For most of them, it was M-1s, Thompson submachine guns, carbines, hand grenades, Browning automatic rifles, .45 pistols, and bazookas.

After several miles of slow, silent creeping, the column stopped at a village. There, they met up with Captain Eduardo Joson, a Filipino guerrilla fighter with a team of eighty men. Joson and his crew protected the column's flanks, guiding the rangers across miles of unfamiliar territory.

Heading out again at dusk, the men, now 200 strong, crossed the terrain in darkness and hit their first significant obstacle—the national highway. Japanese forces used this road, but the rangers needed to cross it. At first, Mucci's men waited for breaks in the traffic then ran across in groups of one or two. Suddenly a Japanese tank appeared, aimed right at them. Captain Prince devised a new plan. Using his map, he found a ravine. The rangers used the gully for cover, creeping under a bridge right beside that Japanese tank.

By 9:00 p.m., every man had crossed the highway safely.

The rangers then marched twenty-five miles, putting them about an hour from Cabanatuan.

They had been awake for twenty-four hours, so Mucci ordered them to rest. Later that night they planned to attack the prison camp.

As the assault commander, Captain Prince was the man who had to come up with a plan to get his team inside the camp, retrieve the prisoners, and get back out—without anyone getting killed.

Prince's job was made even tougher because so many important pieces of information were missing. For instance, how many soldiers were guarding Cabanatuan? How many pillboxes were filled with guns? How many guard towers were there?

And if his team managed to get inside the camp, could these sick POWs even walk?

Captain Robert Prince

The Filipino guerrillas offered what information they knew. Nearby, Cabanatuan city had about 7,000 Japanese soldiers. Another 200 soldiers were even closer, only a mile from camp. And at least 100 Japanese soldiers were inside the camp with four tanks.

"I was very apprehensive," Prince later said. "Any commander's greatest fear is the fear of failure. It preys on you. You have to keep your focus. You have to consider all the things that could go wrong, but then you have to banish them from your mind. If you think about them too long, you can't go forward—you're paralyzed."

As Prince worked on the plan, several surprises arrived.

Without telling Mucci, an American general had ordered his team of Alamo Scouts to do some reconnaissance or "recon"—finding as much information as possible. Equivalent to today's Green Berets or Navy Seals, these scouts were specialized fighters, and they were coming specifically to help Mucci and Prince.

But the scouts had bad news. They told Prince that so many Japanese soldiers were on the road outside the Cabanatuan camp, nobody could get near it.

"The place looks like Main Street in Tokyo," one scout said.

The land around the camp was also challenging. It was so flat there was no cover for anyone approaching Cabanatuan.

But the veteran Filipino guerrilla fighter Juan Pajota knew the area around the camp like his own backyard. He had 90 battle-hardened guerillas and another 160 volunteers ready to help rescue the American POWs.

Pajota went to Prince. He said the scouts' numbers were wrong. There weren't 200 Japanese soldiers nearby—there were 1,000!

And inside the compound there were another 300 soldiers. When Pajota learned that the raid was set for that night, he discouraged it. A Japanese convoy was scheduled to arrive at the same time. The rangers would be crossing the road right when Japanese reinforcements showed up.

Based on Pajota's information, Mucci delayed the raid until morning.

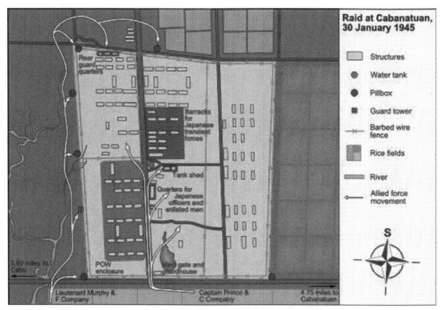

Map of Cabanatuan prison with Ranger directions, courtesy of Jappanlang

Fortunately, the Alamo Scouts had found a shack in front of the main gate. The shack could be used to observe the camp. Some Filipino civilians even offered the soldiers their clothing so the Americans could walk down the road looking like farmers, then quickly slip into the shed.

From inside the shed, the rangers could see the guard towers, pillboxes, and the prison yard.

Prince said they had only thirty minutes for the raid. The plan was to approach the camp with Pajota's men protecting one side and Joson's men on the other. Pajota's group would set up a roadblock near the Cabu River Bridge. At precisely 7:40 p.m., the guerrillas would blow up the bridge, blocking the 1,000 Japanese soldiers from rushing to the compound. Joson's men would block the opposite side, stopping thousands more soldiers from racing over from Cabanatuan city.

The rangers would dash into the camp and rescue the POWs.

At dawn, the rangers began crawling forward on knees and elbows holding their weapons out in front of them for an entire mile. Red ants bit their skin. Mud walls blocked their path, forcing them to climb over them, risking the Japanese sighting them.

Finally they reached the shack. The scouts came out of their hiding places and joined the rangers.

And then, another surprise. More help arrived.

When told of this rescue mission, the American Air Force sent a P-61 "Black Widow" plane to swoop over the camp. The pilot even cut the engine, on and off, making it sound like the plane was about to crash.

The maneuvers distracted the camp guards. They kept looking up at the sky instead of down at the ground as thirty men from F Company moved to the back of the camp.

Their job was to blow up the rear guard towers and pillboxes, along with a barracks of Japanese soldiers. With the attack planned to launch at precisely 7:30 p.m., a lieutenant was going to fire his M-1 rifle as a signal to Prince's men waiting outside the gate.

Prince's men were so close to the camp that they felt exposed. At 7:30, they waited for the shot. Then 7:35. Then 7:40.

Where was the gunshot? What was wrong? At 7:45, the shot cracked the night air.

Front and rear, rangers destroyed the guard towers and pillboxes. Disoriented, the Japanese soldiers were blown to pieces. Rangers shot the padlock off of the front gate and ran into the camp. They raced to their assigned positions. One group took out the officers' quarters. Riflemen raised a wall of firepower. The bazooka team destroyed the tanks.

The rangers blasted open the locks on the POW barracks.

"We're Yanks!" they yelled. "This is a prison break! Head for the main gate!"

But the prisoners, weak and confused, huddled on the floor. Some tried to hide. They thought it was an attack by the Japanese.

"Come on, we're here to save you!" the rangers shouted.

But some POWs still thought it was just another Japanese trick, especially since the rangers were dressed like Filipino peasants. Other men had grown so used to being captives, they were afraid to step outside.

The rangers were also confused.

These POWs barely looked human. They were skeletons, ribs sticking out, legs thin as wooden pegs. Bugs infested their scabby skin. Several rangers immediately tore off their clothing and covered the POWs who were almost naked.

Quickly, they gathered all of the prisoners—some of whom were so weak they had to be carried from the barracks—and raced for the main gate.

The enemy troops, numbering in the thousands, were coming. Time was running out.

They cleared the front gate, and soon the shooting died down to sporadic fire. Pajota's men continued holding the bridge.

Captain Prince, however, stayed behind, going through the barracks, yelling, "Is anybody there?" He didn't want any man left behind. When he received no responses, he finally fired off some signal flares, letting his team know the raid was over.

More than 500 POWs were free.

"I thought we were forgotten," they told the rangers.

Hustling them out of the area, the rangers offered them water and food, including those Hershey's chocolate bars.

Later, this secret mission was called The Great Raid.

Only two rangers were killed. There were no Filipino casualties. But some 500 Japanese soldiers were killed or wounded.

And just as Prince had planned, the raid took only thirty minutes.

WHO FOUGHT?

Captain Juan Pajota

JUAN PAJOTA PLAYED an extremely important part in the success of The Great Raid. Not only did this guerrilla leader have deep

knowledge about the terrain around Cabanatuan, his inform-
ants told him about every movement the Japanese forces made,
including the convoy which would have destroyed the mission
before it even started.

Pajota also took care of small details, such as asking the
local Filipinos to muzzle their dogs so there was no barking as
the rangers snuck past. It's also believed that Pajota might have
come up with the idea to have the American airplane fly over
the camp and divert Japanese attention. And Pajota's troops
held back the enemy during the raid.

"The Guerrillas were our flanking protection at the Cabu
River, which was no more than a mile from the camp," Prince
later said. "There was a sizable force of Japanese, but Pajota
and his men just killed everything in sight that came up that
river and across the bridge. They were the ones that kept this
thing from being a tough deal for us."

Pajota also gathered fifty water buffalo with carts. The animals and carts carried the weak POWs to their newfound
freedom.

BOOKS

*Ghost Soldiers: The Epic Account of World War II's Greatest Rescue
Mission* by Hampton Sides

*The Forgotten 500: The Untold Story of the Men Who Risked All for the
Greatest Rescue Mission of World War II* by Gregory A. Freeman

Unbroken by Laura Hillenbrand

*Resolve: From the Jungles of WW II Bataan, A Story of a Soldier, a Flag,
and a Promise Kept* by Bob Welch

*Pure Grit: How American World War II Nurses Survived Battle and Prison
Camp in the Pacific* by Mary Cronk Farrell and Diane Carlson
Evans

US Army Rangers & LRRP Units 1942–87 by Gordon L. Rottman and
   Ronald Volstad

*Captured: The Japanese Internment of American Civilians in the
   Philippines, 1941–1945* by Frances B. Cogan

INTERNET

Here is an article where Captain Prince talked about the famous raid
   more than fifty years later:
   www.seattlepi.com/local/article/Leader-of-WWIIs-Great-Raid-
   looks-back-at-1181340.php

Historic film footage taken after the raid:
   youtube.com/watch?v=63Fzw6_b7qA

MOVIES

Back to Bataan

The Great Raid

IWO JIMA

February 19 – March 26, 1945

Soldiers of the 1st Battalion 23rd Marines burrowed into the volcanic sand of Iwo Jima as their comrades unloaded supplies and equipment from landing vessels. In the background, Japanese forces rain heavy artillery fire from mountainside caves.

ONE PACIFIC ISLAND remained critical for both Japan and the United States—Iwo Jima.

Pronounced "ee-whoa gee-ma," and translated as "sulfur island," Iwo Jima is a volcanic outcropping about 600 miles from the Japanese mainland. After conquering Saipan, American bombers could take off from that airfield. But enemy forces on Iwo Jima could fire on them, destroying the bombers before they could drop their load.

So America wanted to control Iwo Jima—and Japan knew it.

On February 19, 1945, American military leaders planned the largest Pacific landing to date: 74,000 marines from the 3rd, 4th, and 5th Division formed the V Amphibious Corps or the VAC.

The marines were carried to the black sand beaches by more than 500 ships. More than 100 Corsairs planned to fly in, dropping 6,800 tons of bombs. The navy's ships would then strike the island with 22,000 shells.

With all that firepower, military leaders assumed the Battle of Iwo Jima would be over within a week. Unfortunately, the initial bombardment didn't hit many essential targets. Also, military planners underestimated how many Japanese troops were on the island. They thought there were 13,000 enemy soldiers. In reality, there were 21,000. Still another mistake was made by underestimating the commander of those Japanese troops, General Tadamichi Kuribayashi.

A brilliant tactician, Kuribayashi studied the blunders made by his fellow commanders who had lost Japanese-held islands in the Pacific. Kuribayashi vowed Iwo Jima would be different.

"No man must die until he has killed at least ten Americans," Kuribayashi told his troops. "We will harass the enemy with guerrilla actions until the last of us has perished. Long live the Emperor!"

The American invasion was delayed when General Douglas MacArthur's campaign at the Philippines took longer than expected.

Kuribayashi used that time wisely.

Bringing in engineers from Japan and laborers from China,

his forces dug deep fortifications and tunnels throughout the island. The tunnels had a combined length of *eleven miles*. Kuribayashi stocked them with plenty of ammunition, radios, fuel for vehicles, and medical supplies for the wounded. He also placed his troops on half rations of food and conserved what little fresh water was available.

He planned to force the marines to come to him.

Since he expected the marines to land on the beaches of Iwo Jima, he placed his fire power there to inflict maximum strikes. He planned to allow two waves of marines to come ashore under minor resistance. Then, as the third wave arrived on the crowded beachhead, Kuribayashi would open fire with the deadly power of 65 mortars, 33 large naval guns, and 100 anti-tank guns. He also included some new weapons such as rocket launching aerial bombs and "the Tokyo Express" which consisted of 240-mm and 360-mm mortars with shells the size of fifty-five-gallon oil drums.

Kuribayashi was confident that while Iwo Jima's beaches turned red from the blood of his enemies, he would remain safe, commanding his troops from a bunker located seventy-five feet underground.

On February 19, the American marine invasion force headed for Iwo Jima. Leading the way, the F4U Corsairs started their bombing and strafing runs, providing cover for sixty-eight LVTs armed with forward-firing 75mm Howitzers that followed the navy's rolling barrage from the 14-inch guns on the ships.

Just as Kuribayashi planned, the first two waves of marines met only small arms and limited machine gun fire, so the Americans had little resistance. But the black sand beaches became a huge problem. The LVTs sunk into the soft ground and seawater flooded the engine compartments, stalling the vehicles. With the stalled vehicles in front of them, the third and fourth waves of marines piled up on the beach.

That's when Kuribayashi opened fire.

Artillery and machine gun fire rained from the sky. The Japanese killed more than 2,400 marines.

But the marines didn't stop.

Under that hailstorm of bullets, engineers hit the beach and pushed the wreckage out of the way. They cleared a path for Sherman tanks and heavy artillery to fire back at the Japanese. The 5th Marine Division got close to Mt. Suribachi, the highest point on Iwo Jima, while the 4th Division headed inland to attack the airfields. The 3rd Division was held in reserve.

To escape enemy counterfire, marine rocketeers resorted to hit and run tactics on Iwo Jima

That night, 30,000 marines dug into the volcanic ground to rest—and to prepare for the inevitable Banzai attacks that began with cries of, "Marine, you die!"

But Kuribayashi, the brilliant tactician, didn't use Banzai attacks. Instead he sent out small Japanese patrols to harass the

Americans and gain intelligence on their locations. Kuribayashi also ordered his men to sneak up and kill as many marines as possible during reconnaissance.

The 3rd Marine Division was brought forward, while the 5th Marines began moving inland. Mt. Suribachi was a key objective, rising more than 550 feet above sea level, giving troops the best lookout on the island. On February 23, the hard-driving 28th Marine Regiment, with heavy fire support from navy ships, took the mountain. Amid the dead and wounded on both sides, the marines raised the American flag on the mountain's summit.

Shortly after that flag-raising, an officer ordered one of his men to find an even bigger flag. "Large enough that the men on the other end of the island can see it. It will lift their spirits also."

The marines were facing some of the toughest fighting of the war. They needed a morale boost. This battle was supposed to last one week, but it looked like it was it going to continue much longer—with many more casualties.

Rosenthal's photo of the flag-raising on Iwo Jima

Nearby on Mt. Suribachi, Associated Press photographer Joe Rosenthal saw six men—five marines, one sailor—raising the second, larger flag. Rosenthal snapped the picture. He didn't think much more about it until the photo ran in the American newspapers. It created a national sensation. To this day, the photo of the flag-raising on Iwo Jima is among the most famous wartime images ever. There's even a statue of the image outside the US Marine Corps Memorial near Washington, DC.

As the marines beat their way across the island's bloody landscape, they realized that the enemy had changed tactics. Again. This time they were engaging in guerilla warfare.

Kuribayashi's plans were working.

Just like Saipan, Iwo Jima developed its own "Death Valley." The area was shaped like a bowl with steep sides covered by volcanic gravel that slipped under the marines' boots and made it almost impossible to reach the high spots where the enemy was firing.

The Standard Operating Procedure (SOP) for the marines was to attack in the morning, followed by artillery, demolitions, and then flamethrowers. But soon they realized the Japanese tracked their schedule. Every time the artillery began, the enemy went underground or moved deep inside caves. When the shooting stopped, they came back out again.

So the marines changed the pattern. No artillery fire to alert the Japanese. Also, the marines attacked in the afternoon. Other battalions attacked at night. Though it was slow and costly, the strategy was effective.

The Americans also came up with a new weapon, nicknamed the "Zippo." It was a Sherman tank equipped with a flame-throwing cannon that blasted fire 150 yards and could sustain the flame for up to one minute.

Even with the Zippo and strong air and naval bombardments, the most effective force at wiping out the Japanese positions on Iwo Jima was the ordinary foot soldier.

One by one, these foot soldiers fought their way across the island. Normally, corpsmen don't go on combat patrols, and doctors stay behind at field hospitals. But on Iwo Jima, 827 corpsmen and 23 doctors were killed because of their selflessness in placing themselves in the line of fire to help their fellow marines.

The battle that was expected to last only one week stretched to thirty-six deadly days. Finally, with massive casualties on both sides, the Americans secured the island on March 27.

The Battle of Iwo Jima was over.

Some 6,000 American soldiers were dead. Another 18,000 men were wounded.

In fact, Iwo Jima was the only Pacific battle in which America suffered more total casualties than the Japanese.

Japan lost 20,000 men. About 1,000 of Kuribayashi's men were captured. Most of the wounded Japanese soldiers, following the traditional Bushido code, killed themselves before they could be taken captive.

With America controlling Iwo Jima, bombers needed even less fuel to reach Japan. That meant they could carry heavier bomb loads. Iwo Jima's airfield also offered an emergency landing strip for any B-29 bombers hit during an attack.

Before the war was over, more than 2,400 Army Air Force pilots would land safely on Iwo Jima.

"Whenever I land on this island," said one B-29 pilot, "I thank God and the men who fought for it."

Eighty-two Medals of Honor were awarded during all

of WWII.

Twenty-seven of those medals—more than one-third—went to the marines who fought at Iwo Jima.

WHO FOUGHT?

Two Navajo code talkers in the Pacific WWII

ON IWO JIMA and other WWII battlefields, members of the Navajo Indian tribe relayed military messages using a code based on their tribal dialect. Major General Howard Connor would later say, "Without the Navajos, the marines never would have taken Iwo Jima."

Even Japan's chief of intelligence later admitted that although his men broke the American Air Force's code, they couldn't break the Navajo code. In all of history, the Navajo code stands among a select few that has never been broken.

Iwo Jima produced other distinctive situations. For instance, the youngest Medal of Honor winner ever was Private First Class Jack Lucas who had just turned seventeen before landing on Iwo Jima. During the battle, Lucas threw himself on two

Japanese hand grenades, protecting his fellow soldiers. Though seriously wounded on his right side, he lived to receive the Medal of Honor for bravery and self-sacrifice.

When President Truman himself gave the medal to Lucas, he said, "I'd rather be a Medal of Honor winner than President."

Lucas replied, "Sir, I'll swap with you."

BOOKS

The Battle of Iwo Jima: Guerilla Warfare in the Pacific (Graphic Battles of World War II) by Larry Hama

Island of Terror: Battle of Iwo Jima by Larry Hama

Iwo Jima and Okinawa (World War II 50th Anniversary Series) by Wallace B. Black

Code Talker: A Novel about the Navajo Marines of World War Two by Joseph Bruchac

INTERNET

This website offers many 1945 newsreels reporting on the Battle of Iwo Jima as well as other historic WWII stories. There's also a film clip of the famous flag-raising on the island:
www.watchknowlearn.org/Category.aspx?CategoryID=1865

Find out more about the Navajo code talkers:
http://navajocodetalkers.org

MOVIES

Sands of Iwo Jima

Flags of Our Fathers and its sequel *Letters from Iwo Jima* together present both the American and Japanese points of view.

OKINAWA

April 1, 1945

American Marine on Okinawa, running through Japanese fire

FOR MOST OF us, April Fools' Day means pranks and jokes.

But imagine spending April Fools' Day in landing crafts heading toward an enemy beachhead while bullets zing past your head and explosions blast the water on both sides.

If you survived long enough to actually reach the beach,

you still didn't know if you'd still be alive by nightfall.

That was what April Fools' Day 1945 was like for the American troops landing on Okinawa Island.

Located just 360 miles from mainland Japan, this island would put the American forces right on the enemy's doorstep. But the island had 130,000 Japanese soldiers stationed there, and they weren't about to let the Americans threaten their homeland.

This battle involved more ships, guns, supplies, and troops that any other Pacific battle.

It was also the bloodiest.

Japanese Lt. General Mitsuru Ushijima and his men were desperate to keep the island. Yet oddly, when the first landings of marines came, they were as uneventful as those first landings on Guadalcanal.

Ushijima decided that meeting the heavily armed American forces on flat ground would be disastrous. So his defensive plan focused on Okinawa's southern end where he could use ridges, caves, and hills to his advantage.

However, that plan allowed the marines and army troops to establish a wide beachhead and capture Okinawa's two airfields.

Meanwhile, Ushijima formed two defensive lines that he called the Machinato and the Shuri. Even if he couldn't win this battle, he planned to stall the Americans long enough for Japan to train its civilians for an invasion. All Japanese citizens—old men, housewives, and even children—were taught how to kill American soldiers using kitchen knives, shovels, and sharpened pitchforks. Japan also increased its force of Kamikaze suicide pilots to attack the American naval fleet. Japan was not giving up.

During the second week of April, the American army on Okinawa encountered strong resistance at the Machinato Line. Heavily-fortified Japanese troops had set up cross-firing machine guns for maximum slaughter. They also placed mortars on the reverse slopes—the opposite side of a ridge or hill—so the attackers couldn't see them before they exploded.

At Kakazu Ridge alone, more than 1,000 Japanese troops had dug into the reverse slope. The battle was disastrous.

The Japanese bombarded the Americans with heavy artillery, grenade explosions, and increased machine gun and mortar fire.

But the Americans proved themselves to be incredible warriors. Private First Class Edward Moskala charged forty yards straight into two machine guns, lobbing grenades and firing his automatic rifle. He wiped out both nests. When counterattacks from other positions forced his company to withdraw, Moskala and eight other soldiers volunteered to stay behind to cover the company. During three hours of heavy fighting, Moskala killed more than twenty-five Japanese soldiers. He and the other Americans made it down the ridge to a gorge—only to discover some wounded American troopers left behind. Moskala volunteered to stay with the wounded men while the others found better positions. Protecting the disabled, Moskala killed four enemy infiltrators. When he saw another wounded American, Moskala ran to his rescue. But he was fired on and killed.

Moskala was posthumously awarded the Medal of Honor.

In contrast, the Japanese soldiers showed little concern for their comrades or the citizens on Okinawa. Soldiers used the local people as human shields and murdered others without remorse. Okinawans who survived WWII later gave testimony describing how the Japanese military confiscated their food and executed anyone who tried to hide supplies. Many civilians died of starvation on Okinawa. The Japanese soldiers also told the civilians that the American soldiers would rape and kill them, so many of these people committed suicide. Although some Japanese historians continue to dispute these facts, one of Okinawa's major newspapers reported that the Japanese army gave civilians grenades and ordered them to commit suicide.

As the marines pushed through Okinawa, they discovered people too old and infirm to fight. The Japanese army often executed these people or ordered them to commit suicide. When the citizens met the American soldiers, they were surprised by their humane treatment.

Marine Corporal Fenwick Dunn of Lynn, Massachusetts, shares candy from his K ration with an elderly Okinawan woman

As the fighting continued, the Machinato Line proved difficult to break. General Simon Bolivar Buckner came ashore and added another army division to the fight. Buckner also devised a three-pronged attack—he sent one division straight up the middle of the line while two others attacked from the east and west.

The confrontation led to the heaviest-concentrated artillery bombardment in the Pacific War. The artillery alone fired 20,000 shells with added gunfire from six battleships, six cruisers, and fifteen destroyers. The massive destruction allowed the army to push through an inlet and get a few miles behind the line before flanking it.

By the end of April, the Americans controlled the Machinato Line.

They then moved for the Shuri Line where the battle was locked at Kochi Ridge.

Once again, Ushijima used smart defensive tactics against the American infantry, artillery, and tanks. But his officers wanted to move from defense to offense, so on May 4, the Japanese launched an attack against the Marine 1st Division.

But the marines cut down the Japanese, taking out about 2,000 enemy soldiers.

When Ushijima's counterattack failed on all fronts, he was forced to withdraw his troops, leaving an eight-mile path in the Shuri Line.

At the eastern end of the island, Americans were paying dearly for another ridge called Ishimmi. An army unit of 204 men attacked it, but heavy Japanese fire left them stranded. Following an all-night battle, ammunition supplies ran short. By the third day, when reinforcements reached them, one-quarter of the men were either dead or severely wounded.

The marines were once again tested, this time trying to break through on Dakeshi Ridge. Three days of constant artillery and crossfire allowed them to move forward, yard by yard. Although exhausted, they pushed on from Dakeshi to Wana Ridge and Wana Draw, meeting the same murderous fire. It ripped through the air from a hundred different locations. Bodies covered the ground, but they were irretrievable because of the crossfire. The marines kept fighting.

Ushijima was running low on ammo. He pulled his troops back from Wana Draw and other Shuri lines.

All that remained was a perilous hill called Sugar Loaf, rising seventy-five feet. Another hill named Horse Shoe rose nearby, with Half Moon Hill on the other side. And below these hills was another bowl of death.

The 6th Marine division demolition crew on Okinawa, May 1945

For an entire week, the battle consisted of marines charging up Sugar Loaf and getting pushed back by the Japanese. One night, as the marines were ordered to hold in static defense on the hill, Major Henry Courtney, Jr. made a decision.

"Men," he said, "if we don't take the top of this hill tonight, the Japanese will be down here to drive us away in the morning [but] when we go up there, some of us are never going to come down again."

Courtney asked for volunteers to charge the hilltop.

All forty-four of his men volunteered.

Moving forward, they blasted nearby cave positions and neutralized enemy guns. When they reached the hilltop, Courtney instantly attacked—killing many of the enemy and forcing the remainder to take cover in the caves. Eventually, heavy mortar and artillery fire from the Japanese killed most of the marines, including Major Courtney. He was posthumously awarded the Medal of Honor. His leadership and courageous action contributed to the success of the Okinawa Campaign.

By mid-May, both Half Moon Hill and Sugar Loaf were in the hands of American forces.

By the end of May, monsoon rains turned Okinawa's flatlands into mud pits, which worsened both tactical and medical situations. Vehicles got stuck in the flooded roads. The battlefields were littered with unburied Japanese and American soldiers. Maggots invaded the living soldier's uniforms.

Finally Ushijima was cornered in his last outpost on the end of the island.

On June 4, part of the 6th Marine Division launched an amphibious assault. After several days of fighting, some 4,000 Japanese sailors, including an admiral, committed suicide inside the tunnels beneath naval headquarters.

On June 18, General Buckner was killed by artillery fire. He was the highest-ranking American killed in action during WWII.

Seeing the end was near, Ushijima's chief of staff, Colonel Hiromichi Yahara, asked permission to commit suicide. Ushijima told him: "If you die, there will be no one left who knows the truth about the battle of Okinawa. Bear the temporary shame but endure it. This is an order from your army commander."

Then Ushijima committed suicide by Hari Kari.

In late June, the last of the Japanese resistance finally fell.

The American troops had won the Battle of Okinawa.

It was the bloodiest conflict in the entire Pacific War.

More than 100,000 Japanese troops—and as many civilians—were dead.

More than 3,000 American marines were killed, with 13,700 wounded. The army lost 4,600 soldiers, with 18,000 wounded. The navy lost 5,000 sailors, with nearly 5,000 wounded.

The Allied force also lost more than 400 vessels, damaged or sunk.

But the victory was a decisive win for the Americans. The next step would be an invasion of the Japanese mainland.

Japanese civilians and troops alike were prepared to fight the Americans to the bitter end, no matter how many casualties it created on both sides.

WHO FOUGHT?

BEFORE THERE WAS the internet or satellites or television, Americans learned about what was happening in WWII from newspapers and magazines. Reporters, called war correspondents, risked their lives staying close to the soldiers to bring back stories for their publications.

Ernie Pyle was probably the most famous reporter during WWII. He was also among the first correspondents to focus on the common soldier instead of reporting about the generals or the military's larger developments.

Before going into the Battle of Okinawa, Pyle had premonitions about his own death.

He went anyway.

Just west of Okinawa, Pyle was riding in a jeep with several troops on a small island named Ie Shima. The road was cleared of mines, and hundreds of vehicles had already driven over it.

But Japanese troops suddenly opened up machine gun fire from a coral ridge. Pyle was struck in the left temple. He died instantly. One of Pyle's most famous newspaper stories was "The Death of Captain Waskow."

You can read that column here:
www.pbs.org/weta/reportingamericaatwar/reporters/pyle/waskow.html

BOOKS

Heroes Don't Run: A Novel of the Pacific War by Harry Mazer

World War II Warships by Batchelor

Voices of the Pacific: Untold Stories from the Marine Heroes of World War II by Adam Makos, Marcus Brotherton

World War II Battles and Leaders by DK Publishing

INTERNET

The National Museum of the Pacific War offers more information, including virtual tours of some of its exhibits, such as a Japanese miniature submarine. www.pacificwarmuseum.org/your-visit

You can watch video footage of the Battle of Okinawa, including watching dive bombers attack American ships at the History.com website: history.com/topics/world-warii/battle-of-okinawa

Lastly, check with your parents first before watching this film clip of soldiers fighting The Battle of Okinawa. archive.org/details/0384_Yanks_Battle_for_Okinawa_15_34_45_06

MOVIES

Okinawa: The Last Battle (History Channel)

Hell to Eternity

THE YAMATO

Japan's Greatest Warship

Japanese battleship Yamato under construction, September 20, 1941

LEADING UP TO the attack on Pearl Harbor, Japan built the biggest, most powerful warship—the *Yamato*.

This ship had more than 150 guns. The 9-inch-barrel guns could hurl shells that weighed 3,200 pounds a distance of more than twenty miles—which would be like throwing an entire car all the way into another city. The *Yamato* also had the heaviest armor ever installed on a battleship, pushing the ship's weight to 143,318,000 pounds.

With all these amazing features, the Japanese believed this ship was unsinkable. No gun could penetrate the ship's protective armor. Even with all that weight, the *Yamato* could reach 27 knots or about 31 miles per hour. That was fast for such a large ship.

But oddly, the *Yamato* didn't fight in many naval battles.

After it was commissioned (put to sea) in 1941, it mostly served as a transport vessel for Japanese troops. It did enter some naval skirmishes, but its main battle was The Battle of Samar where it fired its huge guns at the USS carriers *Gambier Bay*, *Hoel*, and *Johnston*, helping sink all three ships.

On March 29, 1945 as the Americans pushed through the Pacific Islands, a conference was held at the Imperial Palace in Tokyo. Emperor Hirohito gathered his military advisors to discuss the American invasion of Okinawa. The Japanese were planning a counteroffensive using 100,000 army troops, 2,000 naval planes, and 1,500 army planes.

Seeing all those ground troops and airplanes, the Emperor asked, "And where is the navy?"

None of the military leaders had told Emperor Hirohito that the American forces had reduced the Japanese navy to only a handful of ships. But his question prompted the military to send out the mighty *Yamato*.

While the American-led forces invaded Okinawa on April Fools' Day, the Japanese devised a counterattack code named Operation Ten-Go. It involved the *Yamato* and nine other ships (one cruiser and eight destroyers) that would sail to Okinawa and attack the Allied forces. Japan planned to run the *Yamato* aground then use it as a stationary artillery platform.

Stocked with ammunition, the *Yamato* sailed for Okinawa. Each of the ships was supposed to take only enough fuel to reach the island. But local base commanders added as much as 60 percent more fuel to the *Yamato*.

Since the Americans had broken the Japanese code, they intercepted radio transmissions and learned all about Operation Ten-Go. Allied ships also saw the *Yamato* heading for Okinawa.

So the American military sent battleships, cruisers, and twenty-one destroyers to try to strike the Japanese before the *Yamato* could get within firing distance of Allied transport ships and landing crafts near Okinawa.

In the early morning hours of April 7, the *Yamato* began shelling Allied seaplanes. American F6F Hellcat fighters came in for support and were soon joined by 280 bomber and torpedo bomber planes. The American destroyers circled the *Yamato*. Suddenly another Japanese ship turned and sailed full steam *away* from the battle, hoping to lure the attackers in the opposite direction. But the plan didn't work—the Americans focused on the *Yamato*.

At 12:41 p.m., two American bombs hit the *Yamato*. They wiped out two anti-aircraft guns and blew a hole in the ship's deck. A third bomb took out the radar room. Five minutes later, two more bombs struck and one torpedo hit the port (left) side. Still more torpedoes hit, taking out the engine room and one of the boiler rooms.

The ship began to flood and list, or lean, toward the port side. The ship's crew began intentionally flooding the ship's starboard (right) side, hoping to straighten her out. But by then, American strafing had taken out most of the gun crews.

When the second attack began, American dive bombers and torpedo bombers came at the ship from every direction, some flying so low they were at sea level. The *Yamato*'s crew loaded the main guns with Beehive shells, fused to explode one second after firing. But three more torpedoes struck the battleship's port side and another hit the starboard side. Water rushed into the ship.

Now the *Yamato* was listing about 20 degrees to port, and the counterflooding wasn't working.

The Americans went in for a third attack. Four bombs hit the ship, wiping out most of the crew manning the 25 mm anti-aircraft guns. Then four more torpedoes hit. More water rushed in. Fires burned inside ship. Basic functions such as lights stopped working.

The *Yamato* was doomed.

An order went out to abandon ship. But much of the crew was trapped and couldn't escape.

A final wave of torpedo bombers struck the *Yamato*'s starboard side while even more torpedoes hammered her hull—the ship's main body.

Finally, the ship lost all power. The last of her guns plunged into the sea.

Three minutes later, the *Yamato* capsized, rolling over with so much force that the suction pulled under crewmen who were trying to swim away.

One final blast came from the ship's magazines. It shot a fireball so high into the sky that it was visible from a hundred *miles* away.

The *Yamato* had sailed from Japan with 3,000 men aboard.

Only 269 survived.

The American airplanes did more than sink the world's most powerful battleship. They ended an era.

Until this time, battleships had ruled the seas. But with the *Yamato* sitting at the bottom of the ocean, everyone realized that planes not only dominated the air, but the water, too.

WHO FOUGHT?

KAZUHIRO FUKUMOTO WAS one of the sailors who survived the *Yamato's* sinking. As fire and explosions took the ship down, Fukumoto jumped into the ocean.

"I have no recollection of the instant I jumped in. But there was a huge explosion—I still remember the sound to this day," Fukumoto said. "Men swimming had their internal organs affected by the impact of the explosion in the water. Men who had hesitated and hadn't jumped in were blown off by the force of the blast...

"We'd jumped off the back of the ship. The ship was still moving forward a little, very slowly, and the propeller was still going bit by bit. I was drawn into the whirlpool from the propeller and pushed backwards. I struggled, but I was powerless—one propeller blade was five meters [sixteen feet] long, so just one turn created a huge whirlpool. I started getting short of breath. I couldn't take it anymore, and I swallowed a mouthful of water, seawater. For an instant it felt better, but there was no air coming in, so I started to get short of breath again. That happened two or three times, and then I began to lose consciousness. At that point, I wasn't thinking about being rescued or what I was supposed to be doing. I was losing consciousness, and I think I was just a step away from death...

"I was clinging to the support beam for about two hours. A man in the distance—I think he was an officer—called for us to come together. I made my way to where everyone had gathered. Men had climbed onto an emergency raft about the size of eight tatami mats [roughly seven by twenty feet]. I let go of the beam and got on the raft. More and more people started coming on, so the raft would go up and down even with the smallest wave. When it got particularly bad, the whole thing would sometimes submerge. We started having to turn people away..."

You can read the rest of Fukumoto's dramatic rescue here: www.pbs.org/wgbh/nova/supership/surv-fukumoto.html

INTERNET

This YouTube video goes underwater to show the sunken *Yamato*, documenting its enormous power and size: youtube.com/watch?v=l5UYt5ih1fc

To see the *Yamato* in 3-D, go to this website: http://3dhistory.de/wordpress/?page_id=27

MOVIES

Yamato

VICTORY OVER JAPAN

August 14, 1945

The telltale mushroom cloud seen from a B-29 Super Fortress during the attack on
Nagasaki, Japan

AFTER HARD-WON VICTORIES at Iwo Jima and Okinawa, American troops were only several hundred miles from the southern tip of the Japanese homeland islands.

The Allies had also formed blockades in the Pacific shipping lanes, keeping supplies such as food and gasoline from reaching Japan.

America demanded that Japan surrender.

Japan refused.

So on March 9, 1945, America launched a night raid over Japan. Three hundred B-29 Super Fortress bombers dropped incendiaries on Tokyo. More than four million people lived in the city. But there were only eighteen air raid shelters that could hold only about 5,000 people each.

As the 17,000 tons of bombs dropped, Tokyo's mostly-wooden structures burst into flames. The bombs contained napalm, a gelatinous form of gasoline that spreads quickly, igniting still more fires.

To escape the inferno, citizens ran to a nearby river, clogging the water.

The bombing killed more than 80,000 people. Once again, America asked Japan to surrender. Again, Japan refused.

You might be wondering: Why would Japan keep fighting when it was clearly losing this war?

There are several reasons.

America was demanding unconditional surrender. That meant Japan would have to lay down all its weapons. As a country, it would no longer have any control or any power.

The Japanese people also considered Emperor Hirohito a god. They worried that the Americans would execute him and inflict "divine condemnation" and national shame on Japan.

Nationalism, in its most extreme form, is where people feel

superior to other countries. Japanese pride had driven the country to start WWII when Japanese leaders felt disrespected in world affairs. Japanese people believed they were a superior race destined to rule over "lesser" people.

All that nationalism and pride blinded Japan to the reality of their hopeless situation. When the Japanese people heard about the impending American invasion, they didn't cower in fear. They armed themselves. They forged bamboo into spears. People strapped dynamite charges to their bodies, hoping for an "honorable" suicide that would also kill many Americans.

Japan's leaders believed that by fighting to the end, they would earn respect and help the country negotiate more favorable terms of surrender.

Another reason was that they feared retaliation from the Soviet Union. Throughout WWII, the Soviets had remained neutral toward Japan—officially. But Soviet forces were stationed along the Chinese border with Japan. Prior to the war, Japan had attacked the Soviet Union. Any unconditional surrender to America would leave Japan vulnerable to Soviet attack.

So despite all the bombings, shipping blockades, starving people, and military battles that were wiping out its own forces, Japan refused to surrender.

America's military leaders planned a radical invasion of Japan.

But everyone knew this invasion would be a major blood-bath—for both sides.

General Douglas McArthur was ordered to lead a two-step assault, code named "Operation Downfall." The first phase would be an amphibious landing on the southern island of Kyushu. If that attack didn't convince Japan to surrender, then a second attack would be launched on the island of Honshu. The invasion was planned down to the smallest details—from food, gasoline, and ammunition supplies for the troops to fighting the civilians who attempted to kill American soldiers.

But "Operation Downfall" never took place.

During WWII, German physicist Albert Einstein had uncovered some scientific theories that led to the creation of a bomb unlike any other bomb.

It was called the atomic bomb.

Einstein had written to President Roosevelt because he was concerned that if Hitler found this scientific information, Germany would make the bomb first. So Roosevelt created a top secret group to pursue Einstein's information. That group was called the Manhattan Project. During WWII, these scientists researched and developed the atomic bomb. (Interestingly, many of the Manhattan Project scientists were Jews who had defected from Germany because of persecution by Adolf Hitler.)

When President Roosevelt passed away in April 1945, his vice president, Harry S. Truman, assumed the presidency. Unlike Roosevelt, Truman didn't think invading Japan was the best way to end this war. America's military leaders were already estimating the invasion would cost more than one million lives—just among the Allied forces alone.

Truman ordered the Manhattan Project to test this new atomic bomb.

Caterpillar tractors haul a test nuclear bomb into the New Mexico desert

On July 16, 1945 in a remote New Mexico desert, scientists exploded the first atomic bomb. It created a distinctive mushroom cloud. The center temperature of that cloud was estimated to be three times hotter than the center of the sun.

"It seems to be the most terrible thing ever discovered," President Truman wrote in his diary, "but it can be made the most useful."

Eleven days after that first atomic test, America once more asked Japan to surrender. If it didn't surrender, Japan would be hit by a new "super weapon."

Once again, Japan refused to surrender.

In the early morning hours of August 6, a B-29 named *Enola Gay* lifted off from Tinian Island in the Mariana Islands.

Piloted by Lieutenant Colonel Paul Tibbets, the plane carried a single atomic bomb named Little Boy. Fourteen feet long and five feet in diameter, Little Boy weighed 8,000 pounds. The bomb contained uranium, a naturally-occurring radioactive mineral, and it was equipped with a parachute to slow its descent, allowing the Enola Gay's pilot and crew to fly away before it exploded.

Just after 8:00 a.m. on April 6, Colonel Tibbets and crew, traveling at 328 miles per hour at 31,600 feet, approached the Japanese city of Hiroshima. Down below, citizens were starting their day.

At 8:11, the bombardier released the atomic bomb.

The Enola Gay banked and raced to safety.

Two thousand feet above Hiroshima, Little Boy exploded.

Within seconds, everything within the radius of the bomb's explosion burst into flames. Glass melted. Buildings collapsed. People were incinerated. The inferno destroyed everything in its path. Further away, people had their clothing vaporized, leaving thread-shaped burn marks on their skin. Their bodies also absorbed lethal doses of nuclear radiation.

The destruction stretched for miles. Thousands of people died. Some death estimates range from 70,000 to more than 100,000 people. Why such a wide difference in numbers? Because the atomic blast destroyed many city records, and because people continued to die for days, weeks, and months as nuclear radiation poisoning took effect.

Once again, President Truman demanded that Japan surrender.

In his public address to the American people, Truman said, "If they do not now accept our terms they may expect a rain of ruin from the air, the like of which has never been seen on this earth…"

Three days later, Japan still had not responded to the demand.

As the Japanese suspected, immediately after the bombing, the Soviet Union declared war on Japan. Troops invaded Manchuria, which was the Chinese land occupied by the Japanese—and Japan's last source for supplies.

With no sign that Japan would surrender, another B-29 took off from Tinian island on August 9. This plane, named *Bock's Car*, was carrying an even larger atomic bomb, called Fat Man. This bomb contained plutonium, another radioactive mineral even more destructive than uranium. Major Charles Sweeney and his crew flew *Bock's Car* to the city of Nagasaki.

At 11:02 a.m., the bombardier released the weapon.

The second atomic bomb killed between 35,000 and 65,000 people and destroyed everything in its path.

Nagasaki, Japan, following the atomic bombing

On August 15, Emperor Hirohito addressed the Japanese people in a radio broadcast.

For most people, this was the first time they had heard the Emperor's voice.

"...the enemy has begun to employ a new and most cruel bomb," the Emperor said, "the power of which to do damage is, indeed, incalculable, taking the toll of many innocent lives. Should we continue to fight, not only would it result in an ultimate collapse and obliteration of the Japanese nation, but also it would lead to the total extinction of human civilization."

Japan surrendered to the United States unconditionally.

World War II was over.

The Japanese people reacted in different ways. Some military officers immediately committed suicide, convinced that self-inflicted death was more honorable than being taken over by their conquerors. Officers who were commanding prison camps pulled out the captured POWs and shot them or hacked them to death with swords. Partly in revenge, partly to avoid having witnesses for war crime trials.

Outside the Imperial Palace, Japanese people wept. To date, Japan is the only country on which atomic weapons have been used. It's estimated that about 200,000 people died in the combined atomic blasts. Historians continue to debate Truman's decision to drop these atomic bombs. Some believe the massive destruction was immoral. Others insist that an invasion would have killed far more people—on both sides, civilian and soldier alike—than all the casualties at Hiroshima and Nagasaki combined.

In fact, the conventional bombs dropped on Tokyo earlier in the war caused far more death and injury than the atomic bombs. Plus, Japan was given multiple opportunities to surrender, with President Truman warning the Japanese leaders about a "rain of ruin" from a new weapon.

Though devastating, most people agree that the atomic bombs probably saved more lives than they took away.

In many Allied countries, August 14 and 15 are celebrated as "Victory over Japan."

WHO FOUGHT?

Captain Oba

JAPAN OFFICIALLY SURRENDERED on August 14. But some Japanese soldiers continued to fight, particularly on the tiny islands in the Pacific Ocean. These loyal soldiers considered surrender shameful. Others didn't believe the news of Japan's loss. Others never heard about the surrender because communications were cut off.

During the Battle of Saipan, Japanese Captain Sakae Oba led forty-six men in guerrilla fighting.

Oba didn't surrender until December 1, 1945.

Dozens more soldiers fought even longer—even through the 1940s, 50s, and even 60s.

However, the very last holdout was probably Teruo Nakamura. He was still fighting the war when he was discovered hiding in Indonesia—in December 1974, more than thirty years after his country had surrendered unconditionally to the United States.

BOOKS

Bomb: The Race to Build—and Steal—the World's Most Dangerous Weapon (Newbery Honor Book) by Steve Sheinkin

The Atomic Bomb: A History Just For Kids! By KidCaps

The Enola Gay: The B-29 That Dropped the Atomic Bomb on Hiroshima by Norman Polmar

Hiroshima by Laurence Yep

The Good Fight: How World War II Was Won by Stephen E. Ambrose

INTERNET

This eleven-minute silent film of archival footage shows the final preparation and loading of the "Fat Man" bomb into the plane that dropped the bomb on Nagasaki. It then shows the Nagasaki explosion from the window of an observation plane. This footage comes from Los Alamos National Laboratory. youtube.com/watch?v=Z9v5sW6t0zI

OCCUPATION OF JAPAN

1945 – 1952

General Douglas MacArthur signs the formal surrender onboard the USS *Missouri* in Tokyo Bay. Behind him stand General Wainwright and General Percival.

THE USS *MISSOURI* sailed into Tokyo Bay on September 2, 1945.

As far as the eye could see, the bay was filled with American naval ships.

On the deck of the *Missouri* stood representatives of nine different nations, each there to sign the documents confirming Japan's unconditional surrender. Japan would be transferred to foreign control and would need to answer to American authority as well as to Great Britain and other victorious nations of WWII.

President Truman placed General MacArthur in charge, naming him Supreme Commander of Allied Powers.

When it came time to sign the papers, MacArthur symbolically placed two men with him on the *Missouri*'s deck: American General Jonathan Wainwright and British General Arthur Percival.

Both generals had spent years in the Japanese POW camps. Their haunted eyes and emaciated bodies testified to the horrors inflicted by Japanese soldiers who showed no mercy to the POWs.

What would MacArthur do?

Would he kill all of the Japanese soldiers who mistreated the POWs? Or would he simply forgive the crimes and tell everyone to get along?

What MacArthur did first was very simple—he fed the Japanese people. They were starving. Food had been scarce for many years.

With its cities bombed out and its government collapsed, Japan had no way to grow and distribute food. So MacArthur created a network and forbade every Allied soldier from eating any food intended for the Japanese people.

Next, MacArthur retained the Japanese government headed by Emperor Hirohito, although it was ultimately under the American's control.

Some Allied leaders disagreed with his choices. But MacArthur lived in Asia for decades and knew Japanese culture. So he refused to try Emperor Hirohito as a war criminal. The Japanese people still saw Hirohito as a god. MacArthur knew that if he condemned the man, it would only increase the shame and resentment among the Japanese people. That bitterness, MacArthur believed, would infect the defeated people and cause them to rise up against any occupying military force.

Unconditional surrender typically allowed the conquering army to strip the defeated enemy of their weapons. But once again, MacArthur knew that it was wiser to allow the Japanese to save their pride and allowed more than five million soldiers who were still alive to disarm themselves.

Then MacArthur earned Japan's profound gratitude by blocking one of its worst enemies—the Soviet Union.

Four major powers were supposed to be part of post-war Japan: the United States, Great Britain, China, and the Soviet Union.

But MacArthur didn't trust the Soviets. So he told Soviet leader Josef Stalin that his country could join in the rebuilding of Japan only if the Soviets also created their own constitutional government. That was a clever maneuver. The Soviet Union was a Communist nation without any democratic principles whatsoever, including basic freedoms of choice and liberty. MacArthur then added a tight deadline.

His plan worked. The Soviets missed the deadline and could not be part of rebuilding post-war Japan.

Japan realized that this fierce American military leader who conquered them in the Philippines was actually looking out for their country's best interests.

When MacArthur arrived at his hotel one day, a line of Japanese soldiers stood waiting. As soon as they saw MacArthur, they turned their backs on him. To Americans, that gesture is a sign of disrespect. But in Japanese culture, turning one's back means you are not worthy of looking directly upon such a great person. They showed great honor to MacArthur who was once their avowed enemy.

However, within the court of justice, MacArthur clenched an iron fist.

After disbanding the Japanese army, he prohibited all military officers from holding any leadership positions inside the new democratic government. He also changed the Japanese rules for owning land, expanded rights for private property, and shifted businesses toward more free market capitalism, so more people could earn more money. With the creation of a new constitution, Japan's Emperor no longer controlled the country. Political power was placed in a parliamentary system, which further increased the rights of women.

In 1945, America placed 430,000 troops in Japan to oversee this post-war occupation.

The next year, the force was cut in half. In 1947, it was cut in half again.

Despite all the bloodshed and brutality during the four years of fighting, even with the ashes of Nagasaki and Hiroshima still evident, Japan showed no signs of rebelling against its new rulers.

MacArthur's leadership was seen as a resounding success. Not only was Japan turned into a democracy, but by 1950, America encouraged the country to re-arm itself.

Meanwhile, an International Military Tribunal delivered justice for the war crimes committed by Japanese soldiers during WWII. These trials continued until 1951, in large part because even the war's most monstrous soldiers received trials in a court of law. Of course, not everyone agreed with providing fair trials for soldiers who refused to obey the most basic parts of the Geneva Convention. But American troops fought and gave their lives in WWII to preserve freedom and rights of all men—even those who had committed horrible crimes.

General Homma, the man responsible for the Bataan Death March, was tried, convicted, and executed by firing squad on April 3, 1946. He was not the only soldier executed after the war.

"It is my earnest hope," MacArthur said, "and indeed the hope of all mankind that from this solemn occasion a better world shall emerge out of the blood and carnage of the past—a world dedicated to the dignity of man and the fulfillment of his most cherished wish for freedom, tolerance and justice."

Today, Japan has the world's sixth largest army. And it is one of America's strongest allies.

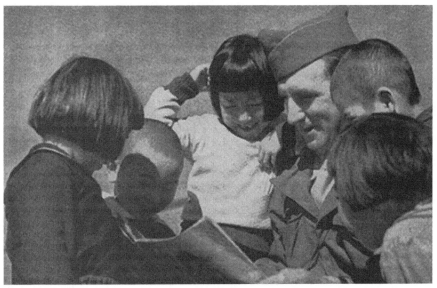

American solider with Japanese children during the Occupation, 1945

AUTHOR'S NOTE

I HOPE YOU enjoyed reading about some of WWII's greatest battles in Europe. And I hope this book is just the beginning of your journey into history.

Even after decades of reading and studying these battles and wars, I'm still learning more about them. Below is a list of books that helped me put together these battles for you.

Someday, you might enjoy reading them, too. Also, look for more books in the Great Battles for Boys series:

Bunker Hill to World War I
World War I
World War II Europe
The Civil War
Ancients to Middle Ages

Be sure to check out my website: www.greatbattlesforboys. com. Drop me a line, or leave a comment on the blog—I really like hearing from you! There's also a Great Battles for Boys page on Facebook: facebook.com/greatbattles

BIBLIOGRAPHY

- *Flying Tigers* by Daniel Ford
- *They Were Expendable* by W.L. White
- *Return of the Enola Gay* by Paul W. Tibbetts
- *The War: Stories of Life and Death from WWII* edited by Clint Willis
- Army Brochure on Aleutian campaign
- *Banzai Attack on Attu!: US Army Combat Engineers in the Aleutian Campaign I* by Del Kostka
- *Military History* magazine
- *World War II* magazine
- *The Capture of Attu: A World War II Battle as Told by the Men who Fought There* edited by Robert J. Mitchel
- *The Story of a Battle* by Robert Sherrod
- *Tarawa: the Story of a Battle* by EB Potter
- *Surviving Bataan and Beyond*, from the manuscripts of Colonel Irvin Alexander
- *Death March: The Survivors of Bataan* by Donald Knox
- *The Rising Sun: The Decline and Fall of the Japanese Empire Vol I* by John Toland
- *The Pacific War 1941–45* by John Costello
- *The War in the Pacific* by Harry A. Gailey
- *10001 Battles that Changed the Course of World History* edited by R.G. Grant

- *Unbroken* by Laura Hillenbrand
- *Ghost Soldiers* by Hampton Sides
- *Japanese War Crimes: The Beast of Bataan* by Peter B. Cook, *American History* magazine
- *The MHQ* (the Military History Quarterly)
- The World War II Database by C. Peter Chen of Lava Development: https://ww2db.com

ABOUT THE AUTHOR

JOE GIORELLO GREW up in a large Italian family in Queens, New York. After hearing firsthand stories of relatives who served in World War II and Vietnam, he took an interest in military history. He teaches a popular class for boys called "Great Battles." Joe's goal is to remind young people that "freedom isn't free" and that history is anything but boring.

You can contact him through his website:
www.greatbattlesforboys.com

And on Facebook:
facebook.com/greatbattles

Find all of Joe's books here:
greatbattlesforboys.com/books